To

_____

From

_____

Date

_____

PROMISES & PRAYERS

for Women

SECOND EDITION

PROMISES & PRAYERS

for
Women

FAMILY CHRISTIAN PRESS
Grand Rapids, MI 49530

The quoted ideas expressed in this book (but not scripture verses) are not, in all cases, exact quotations, as some have been edited for clarity and brevity. In all cases, the author has attempted to maintain the speaker's original intent. In some cases, quoted material for this book was obtained from secondary sources, primarily print media. While every effort was made to ensure the accuracy of these sources, the accuracy cannot be guaranteed. For additions, deletions, corrections or clarifications in future editions of this text, please write FAMILY CHRISTIAN PRESS.

Scripture quotations are taken from:

The Holy Bible, King James Version

The Holy Bible, New International Version (NIV) Copyright © 1973, 1978, 1984, by International Bible Society. Used by permission of Zondervan Publishing House. All rights reserved.

The Holy Bible, New King James Version (NKJV) Copyright © 1982 by Thomas Nelson, Inc. Used by permission.

The New American Standard Bible®, (NASB) Copyright © 1960, 1962, 1963, 1968, 1971, 1972, 1973, 1975, 1977, 1995 by The Lockman Foundation. Used by permission.

Holy Bible, New Living Translation, (NLT) Copyright © 1996. Used by permission of Tyndale House Publishers, Inc., Wheaton, Illinois 60189. All rights reserved.

New Century Version®. (NCV) Copyright © 1987, 1988, 1991 by Word Publishing, a division of Thomas Nelson, Inc. All rights reserved. Used by permission.

The Message (MSG)- This edition issued by contractual arrangement with NavPress, a division of The Navigators, U.S.A. Originally published by NavPress in English as THE MESSAGE: The Bible in Contemporary Language copyright 2002-2003 by Eugene Peterson. All rights reserved.

Revised Standard Version. (RSV) Copyright © 1946, 1952, 1959, 1973 by the Division of Christian Education of the National Council of the Churches of Christ in the United States of America. All rights reserved. Used by permission.

The Holman Christian Standard Bible™ (HCSB) Copyright © 1999, 2000, 2001 by Holman Bible Publishers. Used by permission.

International Children's Bible®, New Century Version®. (ICB) Copyright © 1986, 1988, 1999 by Tommy Nelson™, a division of Thomas Nelson, Inc. All rights reserved. Used by permission.

Cover Design by Kim Russell / Wahoo Designs
Page Layout by Bart Dawson

ISBN 1-58334-236-2

Printed in the United States of America

FAMILY
CHRISTIAN
PRESS

Table of Contents

Introduction

God's promises are eternal and unchanging. But, as every woman knows, life in today's fast-paced world can be so demanding and so confusing that it becomes easy to forget God's blessings and His mercy. This book invites you to slow down and remind yourself of the joys and abundance that God offers to all His children, including you.

This text addresses 72 topics of particular interest to Christian women. Each brief chapter contains Bible verses, a quotation, and a prayer. The ideas in each chapter are powerful reminders—reminders of God's commandments, reminders of God's promises, and reminders of God's blessings.

Being a godly woman in today's world is a daunting task. Never have expectations been higher, never have temptations been so plentiful, and never have demands been greater . . . and that's where God comes in. God stands ready, willing, and able to help you in every facet of your life if you ask Him.

This book is intended to remind you of the eternal promises that are found in God's Holy Word and of God's never-ending love for You. May these pages be a blessing to you, and may you, in turn, be a blessing to those whom God has seen fit to place along your path.

Abundance

The master was full of praise. "Well done, my good and faithful servant. You have been faithful in handling this small amount, so now I will give you many more responsibilities. Let's celebrate together!"

Matthew 25:21 NLT

If you give, you will receive. Your gift will return to you in full measure, pressed down, shaken together to make room for more, and running over. Whatever measure you use in giving—large or small—it will be used to measure what is given back to you.

Luke 6:38 NLT

Now this I say, he who sows sparingly will also reap sparingly, and he who sows bountifully will also reap bountifully.

2 Corinthians 9:6 NASB

My cup runneth over. Surely goodness and mercy shall follow me all the days of my life: and I will dwell in the house of the LORD for ever.

Psalm 23:5, 6 KJV

I have come that they may have life, and that they may have it more abundantly.

John 10:10 NKJV

The familiar words of John 10:10 should serve as a daily reminder: Christ came to this earth so that we might experience His abundance, His love, and His gift of eternal life. But Christ does not force Himself upon us; we must claim His gifts for ourselves.

Every woman knows that some days are so busy and so hurried that abundance seems a distant promise. It is not. Every day, we can claim the spiritual abundance that God promises for our lives . . . and we should.

If you want purpose and meaning and satisfaction and fulfillment and peace and hope and joy and abundant life that lasts forever, look to Jesus.

Anne Graham Lotz

– A Prayer –

Thank You, Lord, for the abundant life given through Your Son Jesus Christ. You have blessed me beyond measure. Use me today and every day to be a blessing to others so that I might share Your abundance with all who cross my path.

Amen

Anxiety

When you pass through the waters, I will be with you;
and through the rivers, they shall not overflow you.
When you walk through the fire, you shall not be burned,
nor shall the flame scorch you. For I am the Lord your God,
The Holy One of Israel, your Savior.

Isaiah 43:2, 3 NKJV

Cast all your anxiety on him because he cares for you.

1 Peter 5:7 NIV

Be anxious for nothing, but in everything by prayer and
supplication with thanksgiving let
your requests be made known to God.

Philippians 4:6 NASB

Let not your heart be troubled: ye believe in God,
believe also in me.

John 14:1 KJV

So don't worry about tomorrow,
because tomorrow will have its own worries.
Each day has enough trouble of its own.

Matthew 6:34 NCV

We live in a world that sometimes seems to shift beneath our feet. Sometimes, trusting God is difficult, especially when we become caught up in the incessant demands of an anxious world.

When you feel anxious—and you will—return your thoughts to God's love. As you face the challenges of everyday living, turn all of your concerns over to your Heavenly Father. The same God who created the universe will comfort you if you ask Him . . . so ask Him and trust Him. And then watch in amazement as your anxieties melt into the warmth of His loving hands.

When you are anxious, it means that you aren't trusting God completely; it means that you aren't trusting God to take care of your needs.

Stormie Omartian

— *A Prayer* —

Lord, sometimes this world is a difficult place, and, as a frail human being, I am fearful. When I am worried, restore my faith. When I am anxious, turn my thoughts to You. When I grieve, touch my heart with Your enduring love. And, keep me mindful, Lord, that nothing, absolutely nothing, will happen this day that You and I cannot handle together.

Amen

Asking God

So I say to you, ask, and it will be given to you; seek,
and you will find; knock, and it will be opened to you.
For everyone who asks receives, and he who seeks finds,
and to him who knocks it will be opened.

Luke 11:9, 10 NKJV

You do not have, because you do not ask God.

James 4:2 NIV

Verily, verily, I say unto you, He that believeth on me,
the works that I do shall he do also; and greater works
than these shall he do; because I go unto my Father.
And whatsoever ye shall ask in my name, that will I do,
that the Father may be glorified in the Son.
If ye shall ask any thing in my name, I will do it.

John 14:12-14 KJV

You did not choose me, but I chose you and appointed
you to go and bear fruit—fruit that will last.
Then the Father will give you whatever you ask in my name.

John 15:16 NIV

*G*od gives the gifts; we, as believers, should accept them—but oftentimes, we don't. Why? Because we fail to trust our Heavenly Father completely, and because we are, at times, surprisingly stubborn. Luke 11 teaches us that God does not withhold spiritual gifts from those who ask. Our obligation, quite simply, is to ask for them.

Are you a woman who asks God to move mountains in your life, or are you expecting Him to stumble over molehills? Whatever the size of your challenges, God is big enough to handle them. Ask for His help today, with faith and with fervor, and then watch in amazement as your mountains begin to move.

God will help us become the people we are meant to be, if only we will ask Him.

Hannah Whitall Smith

– A Prayer –

Dear Lord, today I will ask You for the things I need.
In every circumstance, in every season of life,
I will come to You in prayer. You know the desires of
my heart, Lord; grant them, I ask. Yet not my will,
Father, but Your will be done.

Amen

Attitude

There is one thing I always do. Forgetting the past
and straining toward what is ahead, I keep trying to reach
the goal and get the prize for which God called me . . . .

Philippians 3:13–14 NCV

For God has not given us a spirit of fear and timidity,
but of power, love, and self-discipline.

2 Timothy 1:7 NLT

Keep your eyes focused on what is right,
and look straight ahead to what is good.

Proverbs 4:25 NCV

A miserable heart means a miserable life;
a cheerful heart fills the day with song.

Proverbs 15:15 MSG

You were taught, with regard to your former way of life,
to put off your old self, which is being corrupted by
its deceitful desires; to be made new in the attitude of
your minds; and to put on the new self, created to be
like God in true righteousness and holiness.

Ephesians 4:22-24 NIV

As Christian women, we have every reason to rejoice. God is in His heaven; Christ has risen, and we are the sheep of His flock. But, when the demands of life seem great and our resources seem small by comparison, we may find ourselves exhausted, discouraged, or both.

Today, and every day thereafter, celebrate this life that God has given you. Think optimistically about yourself and your future. Give thanks to the One who has given you everything, and trust in your heart that He wants to give you so much more.

The greater part of our happiness or misery depends on our dispositions, and not on our circumstances.

Martha Washington

— *A Prayer* —

Lord, I have so many reasons to be thankful;
let my attitude be a reflection of the many blessings
I have received. Make me a woman whose thoughts
are Christlike and whose hopes are worthy of
the One who has given me so much.

Amen

Blessings

*I pray also that you will have greater understanding in
your heart so you will know the hope to which he has called
us and that you will know how rich and glorious are
the blessings God has promised his holy people. And you will
know that God's power is very great for us who believe.*

Ephesians 1:18, 19 NCV

*I will bless them and the places surrounding my hill.
I will send down showers in season;
there will be showers of blessings.*

Ezekiel 34:26 NIV

*I will make you a great nation; I will bless you and
make your name great; and you shall be a blessing.
I will bless those who bless you, and I will curse him
who curses you; and in you all the families
of the earth shall be blessed.*

Genesis 12:2, 3 NKJV

*The LORD bless you and keep you;
The LORD make His face shine upon you,
And be gracious to you.*

Numbers 6:24, 25 NKJV

*H*ave you counted your blessings lately? You should. Of course, God's gifts are too numerous to count, but as a grateful Christian, you should attempt to count them nonetheless.

As believing Christians, we have all been blessed beyond measure. Thus, thanksgiving should become a habit, a regular part of our daily routines. Today, let us pause and thank our Creator for His blessings. And let us demonstrate our gratitude to the Giver of all things good by using His gifts for the glory of His kingdom.

Jesus intended for us to be overwhelmed by the blessings
of regular days. He said it was the reason he had come:
"I am come that they might have life, and that they
might have it more abundantly."

Gloria Gaither

— *A Prayer* —

Lord, let me be a woman who counts her blessings, and
let me be Your faithful servant as I give praise to
the Giver of all things good. You have richly blessed
my life, Lord. Let me, in turn, be a blessing to all those
who cross my path, and may the glory be Yours forever.

Amen

Cheerfulness

Jacob said, "For what a relief it is to see your friendly smile.
It is like seeing the smile of God!"

Genesis 33:10 NLT

A happy heart is like a continual feast.

Proverbs 15:15 NCV

A merry heart does good, like medicine.

Proverbs 17:22 NKJV

God loves a cheerful giver.

2 Corinthians 9:7 NIV

A cheerful look brings joy to the heart,
and good news gives health to the bones.

Proverbs 15:30 NIV

*O*n some days, as every woman knows, it's hard to be cheerful. Sometimes, as the demands of the world increase and our energy sags, we feel less like "cheering up" and more like "tearing up." But even in our darkest hours, we can turn to God, and He will give us comfort.

When we earnestly commit ourselves to the Savior of mankind, when we place Jesus at the center of our lives and trust Him as our personal Savior, He will transform us, not just for today, but for all eternity. Then we, as God's children, can share Christ's joy and His message with a world that needs both.

God is good, and heaven is forever.
And if those two facts don't cheer you up, nothing will.

Marie T. Freeman

— A Prayer —
Dear Lord, Your Word reminds me that this is
the day that You have created; let me rejoice in it.
Today, let me choose an attitude of cheerfulness and
celebration. Let me be a joyful Christian, Lord,
quick to smile and slow to anger. And, let me share
Your goodness with all whom I meet so that
Your love might shine in me and through me.

Amen

Children

Therefore you shall lay up these words of mine in your heart and in your soul . . . . You shall teach them to your children, speaking of them when you sit in your house, when you walk by the way, when you lie down, and when you rise up.

Deuteronomy 11:18, 19 NKJV

I assure you: Whoever does not welcome the kingdom of God like a little child will never enter it.

Luke 18:17 HCSB

And he took a child, and set him in the midst of them: and when he had taken him in his arms, he said unto them, Whosoever shall receive one of such children in my name, receiveth me; and whosoever shall receive me, receiveth not me, but him that sent me.

Mark 9:36, 37 KJV

But if anyone causes one of these little ones who trusts in me to lose faith, it would be better for that person to be thrown into the sea with a large millstone tied around the neck.

Mark 9:42 NLT

*E*very child is a priceless gift from the Creator. And, with the Father's gift comes immense responsibility. As parents, friends of parents, aunts, and grandmothers, we understand the critical importance of raising our children with love, with discipline, and with God.

As Christians, we are commanded to care for our children . . . all of them. Let us care for our children here at home and pray for all children around the world. Every child is God's child. May we, as concerned adults, behave—and pray—accordingly.

Our faithfulness, or lack of it, will have
an overwhelming impact on
the heritage of our children.

Beth Moore

— *A Prayer* —
Today, Dear Lord, I pray for all Your children.
This world holds countless dangers and temptations.
I pray that our children may be protected from harm,
and that they may discover Your will, Your love,
and Your Son.
Amen

Christ's Love

And I am convinced that nothing can ever separate us
from his love. Whether we are high above the sky or
in the deepest ocean, nothing in all creation will ever be able
to separate us from the love of God that is
revealed in Christ Jesus our Lord.

Romans 8:38–39 NLT

I am the good shepherd.
The good shepherd lays down his life for the sheep.

John 10:11 NIV

But God demonstrates His own love toward us,
in that while we were still sinners, Christ died for us.

Romans 5:8 NKJV

As the Father hath loved me, so have I loved you;
continue ye in my love.

John 15:9 KJV

Who shall separate us from the love of Christ?
Shall tribulation, or distress, or persecution, or famine, or
nakedness, or peril, or sword? Yet in all these things we are
more than conquerors through Him who loved us.

Romans 8:35, 37 NKJV

Christ's love changes everything. When you accept His gift of grace, you are transformed, not only for today, but also for all eternity.

Christ's love for you is personal. He loves you so much that He gave His life in order that you might spend all eternity with Him. Christ loves you individually and intimately; His is a love unbounded by time or circumstance. Are you willing to experience an intimate relationship with Him? Your Savior is waiting patiently; don't make Him wait a single minute longer. Embrace His love today.

Jesus is all compassion. He never betrays us.

Catherine Marshall

– A Prayer –

Dear Lord, I offer thanksgiving and praise for the gift of Your only begotten Son. His love is boundless, infinite, and eternal. And, as an expression of my love for Him, let me share His message with my family, with my friends, and with the world.

Amen

Contentment

*How priceless is your unfailing love! Both high and low
among men find refuge in the shadow of your wings.
They feast on the abundance of your house; you give them
drink from your river of delights. For with you is
the fountain of life; in your light we see light.*

Psalm 36:7-9 NIV

*The LORD gives strength to his people;
the LORD blesses his people with peace.*

Psalm 29:11 NIV

*Serving God does make us very rich, if we are satisfied with
what we have. We brought nothing into the world,
so we can take nothing out. But, if we have food and clothes,
we will be satisfied with that.*

1 Timothy 6:6-8 NCV

*Let your conduct be without covetousness; be content with
such things as you have. For He Himself has said,
"I will never leave you nor forsake you."*

Hebrews 13:5 NKJV

*E*verywhere we turn, or so it seems, the world promises us contentment and happiness. But the contentment that the world offers is fleeting and incomplete. Thankfully, the contentment that God offers is all encompassing and everlasting.

Do you seek the contentment and peace that only God can offer? Then welcome His Son into your heart. Allow Christ to rule over every aspect of your day: talk with Him; walk with Him; be with Him; praise Him. When you do, you will discover the peace and contentment that only God can give.

Father and Mother lived on the edge of poverty, and yet their contentment was not dependent upon their surroundings. Their relationship to each other and to the Lord gave them strength and happiness.

Corrie ten Boom

– A Prayer –

Father, let me be a woman who strives to do Your will here on earth, and as I do, let me find contentment and balance. Let me live in the light of Your will and Your priorities for my life, and when I have done my best, Lord, give me the wisdom to place my faith and my trust in You.

Amen

Difficult Days

For whatever is born of God overcomes the world.
And this is the victory that has overcome the world—
our faith.

1 John 5:4 NKJV

We also have joy with our troubles, because we know that
these troubles produce patience. And patience produces
character, and character produces hope.

Romans 5:3, 4 NCV

A time to weep, and a time to laugh; a time to mourn,
and a time to dance . . . .

Ecclesiastes 3:4 KJV

They do not fear bad news; they confidently trust the LORD
to care for them. They are confident and fearless
and can face their foes triumphantly.

Psalm 112:7, 8 NLT

I took my troubles to the LORD;
I cried out to him and he answered my prayer.

Psalm 120:1 NLT

Throughout the seasons of life, we must all endure those difficult days that leave us breathless. When we do, God stands ready to protect us. Psalm 147 promises, "He heals the brokenhearted, and binds their wounds" (v. 3 NASB). And God keeps His promises.

Life is often challenging, but as Christians, we must trust the promises of our Heavenly Father. God loves us, and He will protect us. In times of hardship, He will comfort us; in times of sorrow, He will dry our tears. When we are troubled, or weak, or sorrowful, God is with us. His love endures, not only for today, but also for all of eternity.

The strengthening of faith comes from staying
with it in the hour of trial.
We should not shrink from tests of faith.
Catherine Marshall

— *A Prayer* —

Dear Lord, when the day is difficult, give me perspective
and faith. When I am weak, give me strength.
Let me trust in Your promises, Father, and let me live
with the assurance that You are with me not only today,
but also throughout all eternity.

Amen

Encouragement

*Let's see how inventive we can be in encouraging love
and helping out, not avoiding worshiping together
as some do but spurring each other on.*

Hebrews 10:24, 25 MSG

*Watch the way you talk. Let nothing foul or dirty come
out of your mouth. Say only what helps, each word a gift.*

Ephesians 4:29 MSG

*Encourage each other. Live in harmony and peace.
Then the God of love and peace will be with you.*

2 Corinthians 13:11 NLT

*Let the word of Christ dwell in you richly in all wisdom;
teaching and admonishing one another in psalms and
hymns and spiritual songs, singing with grace in
your hearts to the Lord.*

Colossians 3:16 KJV

*But encourage one another day after day, as long as
it is still called "Today," so that none of you will be
hardened by the deceitfulness of sin.*

Hebrews 3:13 NASB

Whether you realize it or not, many people with whom you come in contact every day are in desperate need of a smile or an encouraging word. The world can be a difficult place, and countless friends and family members may be troubled by the challenges of everyday life. Since you don't always know who needs our help, the best strategy is to try to encourage all the people who cross your path. So today, be a world-class source of encouragement to everyone you meet. Never has the need been greater.

We can never untangle all the woes in other people's lives. We can't produce miracles overnight. But we can bring a cup of cool water to a thirsty soul, or a scoop of laughter to a lonely heart.

Barbara Johnson

– A Prayer –

Lord, make me mindful of my words. This world can be a difficult place, and many of Your children are discouraged and afraid. Make me a powerful source of encouragement to those in need, and let my words and deeds be worthy of Your Son, the One who gives me courage and strength, this day and for all eternity.

Amen

Energy

Never be lacking in zeal, but keep your spiritual fervor,
serving the Lord.

Romans 12:11 NIV

Whatever work you do, do your best, because you are going
to the grave, where there is no working . . . .

Ecclesiastes 9:10 NCV

Those who hope in the LORD will renew their strength.
They will soar on wings like eagles; they will run and
not grow weary, they will walk and not be faint

Isaiah 40:31 NIV

He did it with all his heart. So he prospered.

2 Chronicles 31:21 NKJV

And whatsoever ye do, do it heartily.

Colossians 3:23 KJV

All of us have moments when we feel drained. All of us suffer through difficult days, trying times, and perplexing periods of our lives. Thankfully, God stands ready and willing to give us comfort and strength if we turn to Him.

If you're a woman with too many demands and too few hours in which to meet them, don't fret. Instead, focus upon God and upon His love for you. Then, ask Him for the wisdom to prioritize your life and the strength to fulfill your responsibilities. God will give you the energy to do the most important things on today's to-do list . . . if you ask Him. So ask Him.

It's ironic that one of the best remedies for impending burnout is to give yourself away—to pick out one time and place each week where you can stretch out your hands for the pure joy of doing it.

Liz Curtis Higgs

— *A Prayer* —

Lord, when this world leaves me exhausted,
let me turn to You for strength and for courage.
When I follow Your will for my life,
You will energize me. Let Your will be my will,
Lord, and let me find my strength in You.

Amen

Evil

For the eyes of the Lord are over the righteous,
and his ears are open unto their prayers:
but the face of the Lord is against them that do evil.

1 Peter 3:12 KJV

You were taught to leave your old self—to stop living the evil
way you lived before. That old self becomes worse,
because people are fooled by the evil things they want to do.
But you were taught to be made new in your hearts,
to become a new person. That new person is made
to be like God—made to be truly good and holy.

Ephesians 4:22-24 NCV

Submit yourselves therefore to God. Resist the devil,
and he will flee from you. Draw nigh to God,
and he will draw nigh to you.

James 4:7, 8 KJV

Be not wise in thine own eyes: fear the LORD,
and depart from evil.

Proverbs 3:7 KJV

Be not overcome of evil, but overcome evil with good.

Romans 12:21 KJV

This world is God's creation, and it contains the wonderful fruits of His handiwork. But, it also contains countless opportunities to stray from God's will. Temptations are everywhere, and the devil, it seems, never takes a day off.

As concerned Christian women, we must recognize evil and fight it. When we observe life objectively, and when we do so with eyes and hearts that are attuned to God's Holy Word, we can no longer be neutral believers. And when we are no longer neutral, God rejoices while the devil despairs.

We are in a continual battle with the spiritual forces of evil, but we will triumph when we yield to God's leading and call on His powerful presence in prayer.

Shirley Dobson

– *A Prayer* –

Dear Lord, because You have given Your children free will, the world is a place where evil threatens our lives and our souls. Protect us, Father, from the evils and temptations of this difficult age. Help us to trust You, Father, and to obey Your Word, knowing that Your ultimate victory over evil is both inevitable and complete.

Amen

Faith

It is impossible to please God apart from faith.
And why? Because anyone who wants to approach
God must believe both that he exists and
that he cares enough to respond
to those who seek him.

Hebrews 11:6 MSG

Anything is possible if a person believes.

Mark 9:23 NLT

Fight the good fight of faith; take hold of the eternal life to
which you were called . . . .

1 Timothy 6:12 NASB

Have faith in the LORD your God
and you will be upheld . . . .

2 Chronicles 20:20 NIV

When a suffering woman sought healing by simply touching the hem of His garment, Jesus turned and said, "Daughter, be of good comfort; thy faith hath made thee whole" (Matthew 9:22 KJV). We, too, can be made whole when we place our faith completely and unwaveringly in the person of Jesus Christ.

Corrie ten Boom wrote, "There is no pit so deep that God's love is not deeper still." If your faith is being tested to the point of breaking, know that Your Savior is near. If you reach out to Him in faith, He will give you peace and heal your broken spirit. Be content to touch even the smallest fragment of the Master's garment, and He will make you whole.

Faith is the willingness to receive whatever he wants to give, or the willingness not to have what he does not want to give.

Elisabeth Elliot

– *A Prayer* –

Dear Lord, help me to be a woman of faith. Help me to remember that You are always near and that You can overcome any challenge. With Your love and Your power, Lord, I can live courageously and faithfully today and every day.

Amen

Family

You must choose for yourselves today whom
you will serve . . . as for me and my family,
we will serve the Lord.

Joshua 24:15 NCV

Love must be without hypocrisy. Detest evil;
cling to what is good. Show family affection to one another
with brotherly love. Outdo one another in showing honor.

Romans 12:9-10 HCSB

Their first responsibility is to show godliness at home
and repay their parents by taking care of them.
This is something that pleases God very much.

1 Timothy 5:4 NLT

Every kingdom divided against itself will be ruined,
and every city or household divided against itself will not
stand.

Matthew 12:25 NIV

Let love and faithfulness never leave you . . .
write them on the tablet of your heart.

Proverbs 3:3 NIV

*I*n the life of every family, there are moments of frustration and disappointment—lots of them. But, for those who are lucky enough to live in the presence of a close-knit, caring clan, the rewards far outweigh the frustrations.

No family is perfect, and neither is yours. But, despite the occasional frustrations, disappointments, and hurt feelings of family life, your clan is God's gift to you. That little band of men, women, kids, and babies is a priceless treasure on temporary loan from the Father above. Give thanks to the Giver for the gift of family . . . and act accordingly.

What can we do to promote world peace?
Go home and love your family.

Mother Teresa

— *A Prayer* —

Dear Lord, make me a worthy example to all and
a godly example to my family. Give me the wisdom to
obey Your commandments and the courage to follow
Your will. Let me lead my family in the ways that
You would have us go, and let my home be one
where Christ is honored today and forever.

Amen

Fear

Don't be afraid, because I am your God.
I will make you strong and will help you;
I will support you with my right hand that saves you.

Isaiah 41:10 NCV

Don't be afraid, because the Lord your God
will be with you everywhere you go.

Joshua 1:9 NCV

Be strong and courageous, and do the work.
Do not be afraid or discouraged,
for the LORD God, my God, is with you.

1 Chronicles 28:20 NIV

The LORD is my light and my salvation; whom shall I fear?
The LORD is the strength of my life;
of whom shall I be afraid?

Psalm 27:1 KJV

I sought the LORD, and he answered me;
he delivered me from all my fears.

Psalm 34:4 NIV

*M*ost of the things we worry about will never come to pass, yet we worry still. We worry about the future and the past; we worry about finances and relationships. As we survey the landscape of our lives, we observe all manner of molehills and imagine them to be mountains.

Are you concerned about the inevitable challenges that make up the fabric of everyday life? If so, why not ask God to help you regain a clear perspective about the problems (and opportunities) that confront you? When you petition Your Heavenly Father sincerely and seek His guidance, He can touch your heart, clear your vision, renew your mind, and calm your fears.

I have found the perfect antidote for fear.
Whenever it sticks up its ugly face,
I clobber it with prayer.

Dale Evans Rogers

– A Prayer –

Dear Lord, when I am fearful, keep me mindful that
You are my protector and my salvation. Thank You,
Father, for a perfect love that casts out fear.
Because of You, I can live courageously
and faithfully this day and every day.

Amen

Forgiveness

*Have mercy on me, O God, according to your unfailing
love; according to your great compassion blot out
my transgressions. Wash away all my iniquity
and cleanse me from my sin.*

Psalm 51:1, 2 NIV

*If you forgive those who sin against you, your heavenly
Father will forgive you. But if you refuse to forgive others,
your Father will not forgive your sins.*

Matthew 6:14, 15 NLT

*And be ye kind one to another, tenderhearted,
forgiving one another, even as God
for Christ's sake hath forgiven you.*

Ephesians 4:32 KJV

*Whenever you stand praying, forgive, if you have anything
against anyone, so that your Father in heaven
will also forgive you your transgressions.*

Mark 11:25 NASB

*Praise the LORD, I tell myself, and never forget
the good things he does for me.
He forgives all my sins and heals all my diseases.*

Psalm 103:2, 3 NLT

*E*ven the most mild-mannered women will, on occasion, have reason to become angry with the inevitable shortcomings of family members and friends. But wise women are quick to forgive others, just as God has forgiven them.

If, in your heart, you hold bitterness against even a single person, forgive. If there exists even one person, alive or dead, whom you have not forgiven, follow God's commandment and His will for your life: forgive. If you are embittered against yourself for some past mistake or shortcoming, forgive. Then, to the best of your abilities, forget, and move on. Bitterness and regret are not part of God's plan for your life. Forgiveness is.

> Forgiveness is the key that unlocks the door of resentment and the handcuffs of hate. It is a power that breaks the chains of bitterness and the shackles of selfishness.
>
> *Corrie ten Boom*

— A Prayer —

Lord, make me a woman who is slow to anger and quick to forgive. When I am bitter, You can change my unforgiving heart. And, when I am angry, Your Word reminds me that forgiveness is Your commandment. Let me be Your obedient servant, Lord, and let me forgive others just as You have forgiven me.

Amen

Friends

Beloved, if God so loved us,
we also ought to love one another.

1 John 4:11 NKJV

Greater love has no one than this,
that he lay down his life for his friends.

John 15:13 NIV

I thank my God upon every remembrance of you.

Philippians 1:3 NKJV

A friend loves at all times,
and a brother is born for adversity.

Proverbs 17:17 NIV

Iron sharpeneth iron;
so a man sharpeneth the countenance of his friend.

Proverbs 27:17 KJV

We offer a prayer of thanks to God for our genuine friends. Loyal Christian friends have much to offer us: encouragement, faith, fellowship, and fun, for starters. And when we align ourselves with godly believers, we are blessed by them and by our Creator.

As you journey through this day, remember the important role that Christian friendship plays in God's plans for His kingdom and for your life. Christ promises His followers that through Him they may experience abundance (John 10:10). May your friends bless you abundantly, and may you do the same for them.

In friendship, God opens your eyes to
the glories of Himself.

Joni Eareckson Tada

– A Prayer –

Dear Lord, let me be a faithful friend to others,
and let me be an example of righteous behavior to my
friends, to my family, and to the world. I thank You,
Lord, for friends who challenge me to become
a better woman; let me do the same for them.

Amen

Gifts

God has given gifts to each of you from his great variety of
spiritual gifts. Manage them well so
that God's generosity can flow through you.

1 Peter 4:10 NLT

Now there are varieties of gifts, but the same Spirit.
And there are varieties of ministries, and the same Lord.

1 Corinthians 12:4, 5 NASB

Do not neglect the spiritual gift that is within you . . . .

1 Timothy 4:14 NASB

Since we have gifts that differ according to the grace given to
us, each of us is to exercise them accordingly: if prophecy,
according to the proportion of his faith; if service,
in his serving; or he who teaches, in his teaching;
or he who exhorts, in his exhortation; he who gives,
with liberality; he who leads, with diligence;
he who shows mercy, with cheerfulness.

Romans 12:6-8 NASB

Every good gift and every perfect gift is from
above, and comes down from the Father of lights.

James 1:17 NKJV

The gifts that you possess are gifts from the Giver of all things good. Do you have a spiritual gift? Share it. Do you have a testimony about the things that Christ has done for you? Don't leave your story untold. Do you posses financial resources? Share them. Do you have particular talents? Hone your skills and use them for God's glory.

When you hoard the treasures that God has given you, you live in rebellion against His commandments. But, when you obey God by sharing His gifts freely and without fanfare, you invite Him to bless you more and more. Today, be a faithful steward of your talents and treasures. And then prepare yourself for even greater blessings that are sure to come.

Yes, we need to acknowledge our weaknesses, to confess our sins. But if we want to be active, productive participants in the realm of God, we also need to recognize our gifts, to appreciate our strengths, to build on the abilities God has given us. We need to balance humility with confidence.

Penelope Stokes

— *A Prayer* —

Dear Lord, Your gifts to me are priceless and eternal.
I praise You and give thanks for Your creation,
for Your Son, and for the unique talents and
opportunities that You have given me. Let me use
my gifts for the glory of Your Kingdom,
this day and every day.
Amen

Giving

The righteous give without sparing.

Proverbs 21:26 NIV

He that giveth, let him do it with simplicity . . . .

Romans 12:8 KJV

Freely you have received, freely give.

Matthew 10:8 NIV

Do not withhold good from those who deserve it,
when it is within your power to act.

Proverbs 3:27 NIV

The good person is generous and lends lavishly . . . .

Psalm 112:5 MSG

*L*isa Whelchel spoke for Christian women everywhere when she observed, "The Lord has abundantly blessed me all of my life. I'm not trying to pay Him back for all of His wonderful gifts; I just realize that He gave them to me to give away." All of us have been blessed, and all of us are called to share those blessings without reservation.

Today, make this pledge and keep it: Be a cheerful, generous, courageous giver. The world needs your help, and you need the spiritual rewards that will be yours when you share your possessions, your talents, and your time.

As faithful stewards of what we have, ought we not to give earnest thought to our staggering surplus?

Elisabeth Elliot

— *A Prayer* —

Lord, You have blessed me with a love that is far beyond my limited understanding. You loved me before I was ever born; You sent Your Son Jesus to redeem me from my sins; You have given me the gift of eternal life. Let me be thankful always, and let me praise You always. Today, let me share priceless blessings I have received: Let me share my joy, my possessions, and my faith with others. And let me be a humble giver, Lord, so that all the glory might be Yours.

Amen

God's Commandments

Teach me Your way, O LORD; I will walk in Your truth.

Psalm 86:11 NASB

For this is the love of God, that we keep His commandments.
And His commandments are not burdensome.

1 John 5:3 NKJV

My son, do not forget my teaching,
but let your heart keep my commandments.

Proverbs 3:1 NASB

Happy are those who fear the Lord.
Yes, happy are those who delight in doing
what he commands.

Psalm 112:1 NLT

Jesus answered and said unto him, If a man love me,
he will keep my words: and my Father will love him,
and we will come unto him, and make our abode with him.

John 14:23 KJV

*G*od gave us His commandments for a reason: so that we might obey them and be blessed. The Holy Bible contains thorough instructions which, if followed, lead to fulfillment, righteousness, and salvation. But, if we choose to ignore God's commandments, the results are as predictable as they are tragic.

A righteous life has many components: faith, honesty, generosity, love, kindness, humility, gratitude, and worship, to name but a few. If we seek to follow the steps of our Savior, Jesus Christ, we must seek to live according to His commandments. Let us follow God's commandments, and let us conduct our lives in such a way that we might be shining examples for those who have not yet found Christ.

Obedience to God is our job.
The results of that obedience are God's.

Elisabeth Elliot

– *A Prayer* –

Father, Your commandments are perfect and everlasting;
let me use them as a guide for my life. Let me obey
Your Word, and let me lead others to do the same.
Make me a woman of wisdom, and let me walk
righteously in Your way, Dear Lord,
trusting always in You.

Amen

God's Love

Unfailing love surrounds those who trust the LORD.

Psalm 32:10 NLT

For the LORD your God has arrived to live among you.
He is a mighty savior. He will rejoice over you with
great gladness. With his love, he will calm all your fears.
He will exult over you by singing a happy song.

Zephaniah 3:17 NLT

But God demonstrates His own love toward us,
in that while we were still sinners, Christ died for us.

Romans 5:8 NKJV

For he chose us in him before the creation of the world
to be holy and blameless in his sight. In love he predestined
us to be adopted as his sons through Jesus Christ,
in accordance with his pleasure and will . . . .

Ephesians 1:4, 5 NIV

For God so loved the world that he gave his only Son,
so that everyone who believes in him
will not perish but have eternal life.

John 3:16 NLT

Make no mistake about it: God loves our world. He loves it so much, in fact, that He sent His only begotten Son to die for our sins. And now we, as believers, are challenged to return God's love by obeying His commandments and honoring His Son.

When you open your heart and accept God's love, you are transformed not just for today, but for all eternity. When you accept the Father's love, you feel differently about yourself, your world, your neighbors, your family, and your church. When you experience God's presence and invite His Son into your heart, you feel the need to share His message and to obey His commandments. If you haven't already done so, accept Jesus Christ as Your Savior. He's waiting patiently for you, but please don't make Him wait another minute longer.

I am convinced our hearts are not healthy until
they have been satisfied by the only completely
healthy love that exists: the love of God Himself.

Beth Moore

— *A Prayer* —

Thank You, Dear God, for Your love. You are my loving
Father. I thank You for Your love and for Your Son.
I will praise You; I will worship You; and,
I will love You today, tomorrow, and forever.

Amen

God's Plan

"I say this because I know what I am planning for you,"
says the Lord. "I have good plans for you,
not plans to hurt you.
I will give you hope and a good future."

Jeremiah 29:11 NCV

People may make plans in their minds,
but the Lord decides what they will do.

Proverbs 16:9 NCV

There is no wisdom, no insight,
no plan that can succeed against the Lord.

Proverbs 21:30 NIV

Unless the LORD builds a house,
the work of the builders is useless.

Psalm 127:1 NLT

The LORD says, "I will guide you along the best pathway
for your life. I will advise you and watch over you."

Psalm 32:8 NLT

God has plans for your life. Big plans. But He won't force you to follow His will; to the contrary, He has given you free will, the ability to make choices and decisions on your own. With the freedom to choose comes the responsibility of living with the consequences of the choices you make.

Sometimes, God's plans may seem unmistakably clear to you. Other times, He may lead you through a deep valley before He directs you to the summit He has chosen. So be patient and keep seeking His will for your life. When you do, you'll be amazed at the marvelous things that an all-powerful, all-knowing God can do.

God in Christ is the author and finisher of my faith.
He knows exactly what needs to happen
in my life for my faith to grow.
He designs the perfect program for me.

Mary Morrison Suggs

— *A Prayer* —

Dear Lord, let me choose Your plans. You created me, and You have called me to do Your work here on earth. Today, I choose to seek Your will and to live it, knowing that when I trust in You, I am eternally blessed.

Amen

God's Support

The LORD is my strength and song,
and He has become my salvation.

Exodus 15:2 NASB

Finally, my brethren, be strong in the Lord and
in the power of His might. Put on the whole armor of God,
that you may be able to stand against the wiles of the devil.

Ephesians 6:10, 11 NKJV

I am holding you by your right hand—
I, the LORD your God. And I say to you,
"Do not be afraid. I am here to help you . . . ."

Isaiah 41:13 NLT

But my God shall supply all your need
according to his riches in glory by Christ Jesus.

Philippians 4:19 KJV

I know the LORD is always with me.
I will not be shaken, for he is right beside me.

Psalm 16:8 NLT

As a busy woman, you know from firsthand experience that life is not always easy. But as a recipient of God's grace, you also know that you are protected by a loving Heavenly Father.

Do the demands of this day threaten to overwhelm you? If so, you must rely not only upon your own resources but also upon the promises of your Father in heaven. God will hold your hand and walk with you every day of your life if you let Him. So even if your circumstances are difficult, trust the Father. His love is eternal and His goodness endures forever.

No matter what we are going through,
no matter how long the waiting for answers,
of one thing we may be sure. God is faithful.
He keeps His promises. What He starts,
He finishes . . . including His perfect work in us.

Gloria Gaither

— *A Prayer* —

Dear Lord, You are always with me, protecting me
and encouraging me. Whatever this day may bring,
I thank You for Your love and for Your strength.
And I will trust You, Father, today and forever.

Amen

God's Timing

To everything there is a season,
a time for every purpose under heaven.

Ecclesiastes 3:1 NKJV

This is what the LORD says:
"In the time of my favor I will answer you,
and in the day of salvation I will help you . . . ."

Isaiah 49:8 NIV

Humble yourselves, therefore, under God's mighty hand,
that he may lift you up in due time.

1 Peter 5:6 NIV

From one man he made every nation of men,
that they should inhabit the whole earth;
and he determined the times set for them
and the exact places where they should live.

Acts 17:26 NIV

Wait for the LORD;
be strong and take heart and wait for the LORD.

Psalm 27:14 NIV

*I*f you sincerely seek to be a woman of faith, then you must learn to trust God's timing. You will be sorely tempted, however, to do otherwise. Because you are a fallible human being, you are impatient for things to happen. But, God knows better.

God's plan does not always happen in the way that we would like or at the time of our own choosing. Our task—as believing Christians who trust in a benevolent, all-knowing Father—is to wait patiently for God to reveal Himself. And reveal Himself He will. Always. But until God's perfect plan is made known, we must walk in faith and never lose hope. And we must continue to trust Him. Always.

God is in no hurry. Compared to the works of mankind,
He is extremely deliberate.
God is not a slave to the human clock.

Charles Swindoll

— *A Prayer* —

Lord, Your timing is seldom my timing, but Your timing is always right for me. You are my Father, and You have a plan for my life that is grander than I can imagine. When I am impatient, remind me that You are never early or late. You are always on time, Lord, so let me trust in You . . . always.

Amen

The Golden Rule

Do to others as you would have them do to you.

Luke 6:31 NIV

Here is a simple, rule-of-thumb guide for behavior:
Ask yourself what you want people to do for you,
then grab the initiative and do it for them.
Add up God's Law and Prophets and this is what you get.

Matthew 7:12 MSG

Do nothing from selfishness or empty conceit,
but with humility of mind regard one another
as more important than yourselves.

Philippians 2:3 NASB

The one who has two shirts must share with someone
who has none, and the one who has food must do the same.

Luke 3:11 HCSB

And be kind to one another, tenderhearted,
forgiving one another,
just as God in Christ forgave you.

Ephesians 4:32 NKJV

*H*ow should we treat other people? God's Word is clear: We should treat others in the same way that we wish to be treated. This Golden Rule is easy to understand, but sometimes it can be difficult to live by.

Because we are imperfect human beings, we are, on occasion, selfish, thoughtless, or cruel. But God commands us to behave otherwise. He teaches us to rise above our own imperfections and to treat others with unselfishness and love. When we observe God's Golden Rule, we help build His kingdom here on earth. And, when we share the love of Christ, we share a priceless gift; may we share it today and every day that we live.

The Golden Rule starts at home,
but it should never stop there.

Marie T. Freeman

– A Prayer –

Dear Lord, let me teach the Golden Rule, and let me live by it. Because I expect kindness, let me be kind. Because I wish to be loved, let me be loving. Because I need forgiveness, let me be merciful. In all things, Lord, let me live by the Golden Rule that is the commandment of Your Son Jesus.

Amen

Grace

For all have sinned and fall short of the glory of God,
and are justified freely by his grace through
the redemption that came by Christ Jesus.

Romans 3:23, 24 NIV

For the law was given through Moses;
grace and truth came through Jesus Christ.

John 1:17 NIV

In Him we have redemption through His blood,
the forgiveness of sins, according to the riches
of His grace which He made to abound
toward us in all wisdom and prudence . . . .

Ephesians 1:7, 8 NKJV

For it is by grace you have been saved, through faith—
and this not from yourselves, it is the gift of God—
not by works, so that no one can boast.

Ephesians 2:8, 9 NIV

Let us then approach the throne of grace with confidence,
so that we may receive mercy
and find grace to help us in our time of need.

Hebrews 4:16 NIV

We have received countless gifts from God, but none can compare with the gift of salvation. When we accept Christ into our hearts, we are saved by God's grace. The familiar words of Ephesians 2:8 make God's promise perfectly clear: We are saved, not by our actions, but by God's mercy. We are saved, not because of our good deeds, but because of our faith in Christ.

God's grace is the ultimate gift, and we owe Him the ultimate in thanksgiving. Let us praise the Creator for His priceless gift, and let us share the Good News with all who cross our paths. We return our Father's love by accepting His grace and by sharing His message and His love. When we do, we are blessed here on earth and throughout all eternity.

Just as I am, without one plea, but that Thy blood was shed for me. And that Thou bid'st me come to Thee, O Lamb of God, I come! I come!

Charlotte Elliott

— A Prayer —

Lord, You have saved me by Your grace. Keep me mindful that Your grace is a gift that I can accept but cannot earn. I praise You for that priceless gift, today and forever. Let me share the good news of Your grace with a world that desperately needs Your healing touch.

Amen

Gratitude

*Everything created by God is good, and nothing is
to be rejected, if it is received with gratitude;
for it is sanctified by means of the word of God and prayer.*

1 Timothy 4:4, 5 NASB

*As you therefore have received Christ Jesus the Lord,
so walk in Him, having been firmly rooted and
now being built up in Him and established in your faith,
just as you were instructed, and overflowing with gratitude.*

Colossians 2:6, 7 NASB

*Therefore, since we receive a kingdom which cannot
be shaken, let us show gratitude, by which we may offer
to God an acceptable service with reverence and awe . . . .*

Hebrews 12:28 NASB

*I will praise the name of God with a song,
and will magnify him with thanksgiving.*

Psalm 69:30 KJV

*It is good to give thanks to the LORD, to sing praises to
the Most High. It is good to proclaim your unfailing love in
the morning, your faithfulness in the evening.*

Psalm 92:1, 2 NLT

For most of us, life is busy and complicated. We have countless responsibilities, some of which begin before sunrise and many of which end long after sunset. Amid the rush and crush of the daily grind, it is easy to lose sight of God and His blessings. But, when we forget to slow down and say "Thank You" to our Maker, we rob ourselves of His presence, His peace, and His joy.

Our task, as believing Christians, is to praise God many times each day. Then, with gratitude in our hearts, we can face our daily duties with the perspective and power that only He can provide.

A sense of gratitude for God's presence in our lives
will help open our eyes to what he has done in
the past and what he will do in the future.

Emilie Barnes

– A Prayer –

Lord, let me be a woman of gratitude. You have given
me much; when I think of Your grace and goodness,
I am humbled and thankful. Today, let me praise You
not just through my words but also through my deeds . . .
and may all the glory be Yours.

Amen

Grief

When I sit in darkness, the LORD will be a light to me.

Micah 7:8 NKJV

In my distress I prayed to the LORD,
and the LORD answered me and rescued me.
The LORD is for me, so I will not be afraid.

Psalm 118:5, 6 NLT

I have heard your prayer, I have seen your tears;
behold, I will heal you . . . .

2 Kings 20:5 RSV

They that sow in tears shall reap in joy.

Psalm 126:5 KJV

Weeping may go on all night,
but joy comes with the morning.

Psalm 30:5 NLT

*G*rief visits all of us who live long and love deeply. When we lose a loved one, or when we experience any other profound loss, darkness overwhelms us for a while, and it seems as if we cannot summon the strength to face another day—but, with God's help, we can.

Thankfully, God promises that He is "close to the brokenhearted" (Psalm 34:18 NIV). In times of intense sadness, we must turn to Him, and we must encourage our friends and family members to do likewise. When we do, our Father comforts us and, in time, He heals us.

Our tears do not fall without the hand of God catching every one.

Kathy Troccoli

– *A Prayer* –

Lord, You have promised that You will not give us more than we can bear; You have promised to lift us out of our grief and despair; You have promised to put a new song on our lips. Today, Lord, I pray for those who mourn, and I thank You for sustaining all of us in our days of sorrow. May we trust You always and praise You forever.

Amen

Happiness

Always be happy. Never stop praying.
Give thanks whatever happens.
That is what God wants for you in Christ Jesus.

1 Thessalonians 5:16-18 ICB

But the truly happy person is the one who carefully studies
God's perfect law that makes people free. He continues to
study it. He listens to God's teaching and does not forget
what he heard. Then he obeys what God's teaching says.
When he does this, it makes him happy.

James 1:25 ICB

Delight thyself also in the LORD;
and he shall give thee the desires of thine heart.

Psalm 37:4 KJV

How happy are those who can live in your house,
always singing your praises.
How happy are those who are strong in the Lord . . . .

Psalm 84:4, 5 NLT

Do you seek happiness, abundance, and contentment? If so, here are some things you should do: Love God and His Son; depend upon God for strength; try, to the best of your abilities, to follow God's will; and strive to obey His Holy Word. When you do these things, you'll discover that happiness goes hand-in-hand with righteousness. The happiest people are not those who rebel against God; the happiest people are those who love God and obey His commandments.

We will never be happy until we make God
the source of our fulfillment and
the answer to our longings.

Stormie Omartian

– A Prayer –

Lord, let me be a woman who celebrates life.
Let me rejoice in the gift of this day,
and let me praise You for the gift of Your Son.
Let me be a joyful Christian, Lord,
as I share Your Good News with friends,
with family, and with the world.

Amen

Holy Living

You will teach me how to live a holy life.
Being with you will fill me with joy;
at your right hand I will find pleasure forever.

Psalm 16:11 NCV

But now you must be holy in everything you do,
just as God—who chose you to be his children—is holy.
For he himself has said,
"You must be holy because I am holy."

1 Peter 1:15, 16 NLT

Blessed are those who hunger and thirst for righteousness,
for they will be filled.

Matthew 5:6 NIV

The LORD rewarded me according to my righteousness . . . .

Psalm 18:20 KJV

The righteous shall flourish like the palm tree:
he shall grow like a cedar in Lebanon.

Psalm 92:12 KJV

*E*veryday life is an adventure in decision-making. Each day, we make countless decisions that hopefully bring us closer to God. When we live according to God's commandments, we share in His abundance and His peace. But, when we turn our backs upon God by disobeying Him, we bring needless suffering upon ourselves and upon our families.

Do you seek God's peace and His blessings? Then strive to live a holy life that is pleasing to Him. When you're faced with a difficult choice or a powerful temptation, seek God's counsel and trust the counsel He gives. Invite God into your heart and live according to His commandments. When you do, you will be blessed today, and tomorrow, and forever.

Be faithful in the little practices of love which will build in you the life of holiness and will make you Christlike.

Mother Teresa

– *A Prayer* –

Lord, You are a righteous and Holy God, and You have called me to be a righteous woman. When I fall short, forgive me and renew a spirit of holiness within me. Lead me, Lord, along Your path, and guide me far from the temptations of this world. Let Your Holy Word guide my actions, and let Your love reside in my heart, this day and every day.

Amen

Hope

Let us hold on to the confession of our hope
without wavering, for He who promised is faithful.

Hebrews 10:23 HCSB

For I hope in You, O LORD;
You will answer, O Lord my God.

Psalm 38:15 NASB

The LORD is good to those whose hope is in him,
to the one who seeks him; it is good to wait quietly
for the salvation of the LORD.

Lamentations 3:25, 26 NIV

May the God of hope fill you with all joy and peace as you
trust in him, so that you may overflow with hope
by the power of the Holy Spirit.

Romans 15:13 NIV

Now faith is the substance of things hoped for,
the evidence of things not seen.

Hebrews 11:1 KJV

The hope that the world offers is fleeting and imperfect. The hope that God offers is unchanging, unshakable, and unending. It is no wonder, then, that when we seek security from worldly sources, our hopes are often dashed. Thankfully, God has no such record of failure.

Even though this world can be a place of trials and struggles, God's promises are eternal and unchanging. So today, as you embark upon the next stage of your life's journey, consider the words of the Psalmist: "You are my hope; O Lord GOD, You are my confidence" (71:5 NASB). Then, place your trust in the One who cannot be shaken.

The most profane word we use is "hopeless."
When you say a situation or person is hopeless,
you are slamming the door in the face of God.

Kathy Troccoli

— *A Prayer* —

Dear Lord, make me a woman of hope. If I become discouraged, let me turn to You. If I grow weary, let me seek strength in You. When I face disappointments, let me seek Your will and trust Your Word.
In every aspect of my life, I will trust You, Father, so that my heart will be filled with faith and hope, this day and forever.

Amen

The Impossible

But as it is written: "Eye has not seen, nor ear heard,
nor have entered into the heart of man the things
which God has prepared for those who love Him."

1 Corinthians 2:9 NKJV

But Jesus looked at them and said to them,
"With men this is impossible,
but with God all things are possible."

Matthew 19:26 NKJV

God also testified to it [salvation] by signs,
wonders and various miracles, and gifts of the Holy Spirit
distributed according to his will.

Hebrews 2:4 NIV

Jesus said to them,
"I have shown you many great miracles from the Father."

John 10:32 NIV

You are the God who performs miracles;
you display your power among the peoples.

Psalm 77:14 NIV

*D*o you believe in an all-powerful God who can do miraculous things in you and through you? You should. But perhaps, as you have faced the inevitable struggles of life here on earth, you have—without realizing it—placed limitations on God. To do so is a profound mistake.

Since the moment that He created our universe out of nothingness, God has made a habit of doing miraculous things. And He still works miracles today. Expect Him to work miracles in your own life, and then be watchful. With God, absolutely nothing is impossible, including an amazing assortment of miracles that He stands ready, willing, and able to perform for you and yours.

Faith sees the invisible, believes the unbelievable,
and receives the impossible.

Corrie ten Boom

— A Prayer —

Dear Lord, absolutely nothing is impossible for You.
Let me trust in Your power and in Your miracles.
When I lose hope, give me faith; when others lose hope,
let me tell them of Your glorious works.
Today, Lord, keep me mindful that You are
a God of infinite possibilities and infinite love.

Amen

Integrity

Till I die, I will not deny my integrity.
I will maintain my righteousness and never let go of it;
my conscience will not reproach me as long as I live.

Job 27:5, 6 NIV

May integrity and uprightness protect me,
because my hope is in you.

Psalm 25:21 NIV

In everything set them an example by doing what is good.
In your teaching show integrity, seriousness and
soundness of speech that cannot be condemned,
so that those who oppose you may be ashamed
because they have nothing bad to say about us.

Titus 2:7-8 NIV

A good name is to be chosen rather than great riches,
loving favor rather than silver and gold.

Proverbs 22:1 NKJV

The integrity of the upright shall guide them . . . .

Proverbs 11:3 KJV

Wise women understand that integrity is a crucial building block in the foundation of a well-lived life. Integrity is built slowly over a lifetime. It is the sum of every right decision, every honest word, every noble thought, and every heartfelt prayer. It is forged on the anvil of honorable work and polished by the twin virtues of generosity and humility. Integrity is a precious thing—difficult to build, but easy to tear down; godly women value it and protect it at all costs.

God never called us to naïveté.
He called us to integrity . . . . The biblical concept
of integrity emphasizes mature innocence
not childlike ignorance.

Beth Moore

– A Prayer –

Lord, You are a God of integrity; let me be a woman of integrity. Sometimes speaking the truth is difficult, but when I am weak or fearful, Lord, give me the strength to speak words that are worthy of the One who created me, so that others might see Your eternal truth reflected in my words and my deeds.

Amen

Jesus

*In the beginning was the Word, and the Word was with God,
and the Word was God . . . . And the Word was made flesh,
and dwelt among us, (and we beheld his glory, the glory as of
the only begotten of the Father,) full of grace and truth.*

John 1:1, 14 KJV

*"For Jesus is the one referred to in the Scriptures,
where it says, 'The stone that you builders rejected has now
become the cornerstone.' There is salvation in no one else!
There is no other name in all of heaven
for people to call on to save them."*

Acts 4:11, 12 NLT

*Let us run with endurance the race that is set before us,
fixing our eyes on Jesus, the author and perfecter of faith,
who for the joy set before Him endured the cross,
despising the shame, and has sat down at
the right hand of the throne of God.*

Hebrews 12:1, 2 NASB

Jesus Christ the same yesterday, and today, and for ever.

Hebrews 13:8 KJV

*O*ur circumstances change but Jesus does not. Even when the world seems to be trembling beneath our feet, Jesus remains the spiritual bedrock that cannot be moved.

The old familiar hymn begins, "What a friend we have in Jesus . . . ." No truer words were ever penned. Jesus is the sovereign friend and ultimate savior of mankind. Christ showed enduring love for His believers by willingly sacrificing His own life so that we might have eternal life. Let us love Him, praise Him, and share His message of salvation with our neighbors and with the world.

Jesus makes God visible.
But that truth does not make Him somehow
less than God. He is equally supreme with God.

Anne Graham Lotz

— *A Prayer* —
Dear Lord, today I will abide in Jesus. I will look to Him as my Savior, and I will follow in His footsteps. I will strive to please Him, and I will separate myself from evils of this world. Thank You, Lord, for Your Son. Today, I will count Him as my dearest friend, and I will share His transforming message with a world in desperate need of His peace.

Amen

Joy

These things I have spoken to you, that My joy
may remain in you, and that your joy may be full.

John 15:11 NKJV

A joyful heart is good medicine,
but a broken spirit dries up the bones.

Proverbs 17:22 NASB

Always be full of joy in the Lord. I say it again—rejoice!

Philippians 4:4 NLT

Rejoice, and be exceeding glad:
for great is your reward in heaven . . . .

Matthew 5:12 KJV

Shout for joy to the LORD, all the earth.
Worship the LORD with gladness;
come before him with joyful songs.

Psalm 100:1, 2 NIV

So now we can rejoice in our wonderful new relationship
with God—all because of what our Lord Jesus Christ has
done for us in making us friends of God.

Romans 5:11 NLT

*J*oni Eareckson Tada spoke for Christian women of every generation when she observed, "I wanted the deepest part of me to vibrate with that ancient yet familiar longing, that desire for something that would fill and overflow my soul."

God's Word makes it clear: He intends that His joy should become our joy. The Lord intends that believers should share His love with His joy in their hearts. Yet sometimes, amid the inevitable hustle and bustle of life here on earth, we can forfeit—albeit temporarily—God's joy as we wrestle with the challenges of daily living.

If, today, your heart is heavy, open the door of your soul to Christ. He will give you peace and joy. And if you already have the joy of Christ in your heart, share it freely, just as Christ freely shared His joy with you.

Finding joy means first of all finding Jesus.

Jill Briscoe

– *A Prayer* –
Lord, make me a joyous Christian.
Because of my salvation through Your Son,
I have every reason to celebrate life. Let me share the
joyful news of Jesus Christ, and let my life be
a testimony to His love and to His grace.

Amen

Judging Others

*You, therefore, have no excuse, you who pass judgment
on someone else, for at whatever point you judge the other,
you are condemning yourself.*

Romans 2:1 NIV

*Judge not, and ye shall not be judged: condemn not,
and ye shall not be condemned . . . .*

Luke 6:37 KJV

*Do not judge, or you too will be judged.
For in the same way you judge others, you will be judged,
and with the measure you use, it will be measured to you.*

Matthew 7:1, 2 NIV

*Why do you look at the speck of sawdust in your brother's
eye and pay no attention to the plank in your own eye?
How can you say to your brother, "Let me take the speck
out of your eye," when all the time there is a plank in
your own eye? You hypocrite, first take the plank out of
your own eye, and then you will see clearly to remove
the speck from your brother's eye.*

Matthew 7:3-5 NIV

*E*ven the most devoted Christians may fall prey to a powerful yet subtle temptation: the temptation to judge others. But as believers, we are commanded to refrain from such behavior. The warning of Matthew 7:1 is clear: "Judge not, that ye be not judged" (KJV).

We have all fallen short of God's commandments, and He has forgiven us. We, too, must forgive others. And, we must refrain from judging them. As Christian believers, we are warned that to judge others is to invite fearful consequences: To the extent we judge others, so, too, will we be judged by God. Let us refrain, then, from judging our neighbors. Instead, let us forgive them and love them in the same way that God has forgiven us.

How often should you forgive the other person?
Only as many times as you want God to forgive you!
Marie T. Freeman

– *A Prayer* –
Lord, it's so easy to judge other people,
but it's also easy to misjudge them. Only You can judge
a human heart, Lord, so let me love my friends
and neighbors, and let me help them,
but never let me judge them.
Amen

Kindness

Show respect for all people.
Love the brothers and sisters of God's family.

1 Peter 2:17 ICB

May the Lord cause you to increase
and abound in love for one another, and for all people.

1 Thessalonians 3:12 NASB

And be ye kind one to another, tenderhearted,
forgiving one another,
even as God for Christ's sake hath forgiven you.

Ephesians 4:32 KJV

Verily I say unto you,
Inasmuch as ye have done it unto one of the least of these
my brethren, ye have done it unto me.

Matthew 25:40 KJV

Be ye therefore merciful, as your Father also is merciful.

Luke 6:36 KJV

Where does kindness start? It starts in our hearts and works its way out from there. Jesus taught us that a pure heart is a wonderful blessing. It's up to each of us to fill our hearts with love for God, love for Jesus, and love for all people. When we do, we are blessed.

Today, invite the love of Christ into your heart and share His love with your family and friends. And remember that enduring kindness always comes from a pure heart . . . like yours!

The nicest thing we can do for our heavenly Father
is to be kind to one of His children.

St. Teresa of Avila

– A Prayer –

Help me, Lord, to see the needs of those around me.
Today, let me show mercy to those who cross my path.
Today, let me spread kind words of thanksgiving and
celebration in honor of Your Son. Today, let forgiveness
rule my heart. And every day, Lord, let my love for
Christ be reflected through deeds of kindness for those
who need the healing touch of the Master's hand.

Amen

Laughter

*There is a time for everything, and a season for every activity
under heaven . . . a time to weep and a time to laugh,
a time to mourn and a time to dance . . . .*

Ecclesiastes 3:1, 4 NIV

A happy heart is like good medicine.

Proverbs 17:22 NCV

*Shout for joy to the LORD, all the earth, burst into jubilant
song with music; make music to the LORD with the harp, with
the harp and the sound of singing,
with trumpets and the blast of the ram's horn—
shout for joy before the LORD, the King.*

Psalm 98:4-6 NIV

*Nehemiah said, "Go and enjoy choice food and sweet drinks,
and send some to those who have nothing prepared.
This day is sacred to our Lord.
Do not grieve, for the joy of the LORD is your strength."*

Nehemiah 8:10 NIV

*I*t has been said, quite correctly, that laughter is God's medicine. But sometimes, amid the stresses of the day, we forget to take our medicine. Instead of viewing our world with a mixture of optimism and humor, we allow worries and distractions to rob us of the joy that God intends for our lives.

Today, as you go about your daily activities, approach life with a smile and a chuckle. After all, God created laughter for a reason . . . and Father indeed knows best. So laugh!

> Humor is a prelude to faith,
> and laughter is the beginning of prayer.
>
> *Reinhold Niebuhr*

– A Prayer –

Dear Lord, laughter is Your gift. Today and every day,
put a smile on my face, and let me share
that smile with all who cross my path . . .
and let me laugh.

Amen

Learning

A wise person pays attention to correction
that will improve his life.

Proverbs 15:31 ICB

Remember what you are taught,
and listen carefully to words of knowledge.

Proverbs 23:12 NCV

The fear of the Lord is the beginning of knowledge,
but fools despise wisdom and discipline.

Proverbs 1:7 NIV

The knowledge of the secrets of the kingdom of heaven
has been given to you . . . .

Matthew 13:11 NIV

It is not good to have zeal without knowledge,
nor to be hasty and miss the way.

Proverbs 19:2 NIV

If we are to grow as Christians and as women, we need both knowledge and wisdom. Knowledge is found in textbooks. Wisdom, on the other hand, is found in God's Holy Word and in the carefully-chosen words of loving parents, family members, and friends. Knowledge is an important building block in a well-lived life, and it pays rich dividends both personally and professionally. But wisdom is even more important because it refashions not only the mind, but also the heart.

Our first step toward gaining God's wisdom is to know
what we do not know; that is,
to be aware of our shortcomings.

Dianna Booher

— A Prayer —

Dear Lord, I have lots to learn. Help me to watch,
to listen, to think, and to learn, every day of my life.

Amen

Loving God

By this we know that we love the children of God,
when we love God and keep His commandments.

1 John 5:2 NKJV

If you love me, you will obey what I command.

John 14:15 NIV

Jesus replied, "'Love the Lord your God with all your heart
and with all your soul and with all your mind.'
This is the first and greatest commandment. And the second
is like it: 'Love your neighbor as yourself.'
All the Law and the Prophets hang on these
two commandments."

Matthew 22:37-40 NIV

We love him, because he first loved us.

1 John 4:19 KJV

I will sing of the LORD's great love forever;
with my mouth I will make your faithfulness
known through all generations.

Psalm 89:1 NIV

When we worship God with faith and assurance, when we place Him at the absolute center of our lives, we invite His love into our hearts. In turn, we grow to love Him more deeply as we sense His love for us.

St. Augustine wrote, "I love you, Lord, not doubtingly, but with absolute certainty. Your Word beat upon my heart until I fell in love with you, and now the universe and everything in it tells me to love you." Let us pray that we, too, will turn our hearts to our Father, knowing with certainty that He loves us and that we love Him.

If you love God enough to ask Him what you can do for Him, then your relationship is growing deep.

Stormie Omartian

— *A Prayer* —

Dear God, let me share Your love with the world. Make me a woman of compassion. Help me to recognize the needs of others. Let me forgive those who have hurt me, just as You have forgiven me. And let the love of Your Son shine in me and through me today, tomorrow, and throughout all eternity.

Amen

Loving Others

Love each other like brothers and sisters.
Give each other more honor than you want for yourselves.

Romans 12:10 NCV

I give you a new commandment: that you love one another.
Just as I have loved you, you should also love one another.
By this all people will know that you are My disciples,
if you have love for one another.

John 13:34, 35 HCSB

And the Lord make you to increase
and abound in love one toward another,
and toward all men . . . .

1 Thessalonians 3:12 KJV

Now these three remain: faith, hope, and love.
But the greatest of these is love.

1 Corinthians 13:13 HCSB

The beautiful words of 1st Corinthians 13 remind us that love is God's commandment: Faith is important, of course. So, too, is hope. But, love is more important still. We are commanded (not advised, not encouraged . . . commanded!) to love one another just as Christ loved us (John 13:34). That's a tall order, but as Christians, we are obligated to follow it.

Christ showed His love for us on the cross, and we are called upon to return Christ's love by sharing it. Today, let us spread Christ's love to families, friends, students and strangers, so that through us, others might come to know Him.

There are only two duties required of us—the love of God and the love of our neighbor, and the surest sign of discovering whether we observe these duties is the love of our neighbor.

St. Teresa of Avila

– *A Prayer* –

Dear Lord, Your love for me is infinite and eternal. Let me acknowledge Your love, accept Your love, and share Your love. Make me a woman of compassion, understanding, and forgiveness. And let the love that I feel in my heart be expressed through kind words, good deeds and heartfelt prayers.

Amen

Materialism

For where your treasure is, there your heart will be also.

Luke 12:34 NKJV

He who trusts in his riches will fall,
but the righteous will flourish . . . .

Proverbs 11:28 NKJV

No one can serve two masters.
The person will hate one master and love the other,
or will follow one master and refuse to follow the other.
You cannot serve both God and worldly riches.

Matthew 6:24 NCV

A man's life does not consist in the abundance
of his possessions.

Luke 12:15 NIV

Yes, a person is a fool to store up earthly wealth
but not have a rich relationship with God.

Luke 12:21 NLT

*I*n the demanding world in which we live, financial prosperity can be a good thing, but spiritual prosperity is profoundly more important. Yet our society leads us to believe otherwise. The world glorifies material possessions, personal fame, and physical beauty above all else; these things, of course, are totally unimportant to God. God sees the human heart, and that's what is important to Him.

The world will do everything it can to convince you that "things" are important. The world will tempt you to value fortune above faith and possessions above peace. God, on the other hand, will try to convince you that your relationship with Him is all-important. Trust God.

We are made spiritually lethargic
by a steady diet of materialism.

Mary Morrison Suggs

— *A Prayer* —

Lord, my greatest possession is my relationship with You through Jesus Christ. You have promised that, when I first seek Your Kingdom and Your righteousness, You will give me whatever I need. Let me trust You completely, Lord, for my needs, both material and spiritual, this day and always.

Amen

Maturity

When I was a child, I spoke and thought and reasoned as
a child does. But when I grew up, I put away childish things.

1 Corinthians 13:11 NLT

Consider it pure joy, my brothers, whenever you face trials
of many kinds, because you know that the testing of your
faith develops perseverance. Perseverance must
finish its work so that you may be mature and complete,
not lacking anything.

James 1:2-4 NIV

But grow in the grace and knowledge of
our Lord and Savior Jesus Christ.

2 Peter 3:18 NIV

Therefore let us leave the elementary teachings
about Christ and go on to maturity . . . .

Hebrews 6:1 NIV

There has never been the slightest doubt in my mind that
the God who started this great work in you would keep
at it and bring it to a flourishing finish on
the very day Christ Jesus appears.

Philippians 1:6 MSG

The journey toward spiritual maturity lasts a lifetime. As Christians, we can and should continue to grow in the love and the knowledge of our Savior as long as we live.

Life is a series of choices and decisions. Each day, we make countless decisions that can bring us closer to God . . . or not. When we live according to the principles contained in God's Holy Word, we embark upon a journey of spiritual growth that results in life abundant and life eternal.

We cannot hope to reach Christian maturity
in any way other than by yielding ourselves utterly
and willingly to His mighty working.

Hannah Whitall Smith

– A Prayer –

Thank You, Lord, that I am not yet what I am to become. The Holy Scripture tells me that You are at work in my life, continuing to help me grow and to mature in the faith. Show me Your wisdom, Father, and let me live according to Your Word and Your will.

Amen

Mistakes

Have mercy on me, O God, according to your unfailing
love; according to your great compassion blot
out my transgressions. Wash away all my iniquity
and cleanse me from my sin.

Psalm 51:1, 2 NIV

I waited patiently for the LORD; he turned to me and
heard my cry. He lifted me out of the slimy pit,
out of the mud and mire; he set my feet on a rock and
gave me a firm place to stand. He put a new song in
my mouth, a hymn of praise to our God . . . .

Psalm 40:1-3 NIV

You were taught, with regard to your former way of life, to
put off your old self, which is being corrupted by its deceitful
desires; to be made new in the attitude of your minds;
and to put on the new self, created to be like
God in true righteousness and holiness.

Ephesians 4:22-24 NIV

If we confess our sins, he is faithful and just
and will forgive us our sins
and purify us from all unrighteousness.

1 John 1:9 NIV

The words are all too familiar and all too true: "To err is human . . . ." Yes, we human beings are inclined to make mistakes, and lots of them.

We are imperfect women living in an imperfect world; mistakes are simply part of the price we pay for being here. But, even though mistakes are an inevitable part of life's journey, repeated mistakes should not be. When we commit the inevitable blunders of life, we must correct them, learn from them, and pray to God for the wisdom not to repeat them. And then, if we are successful, our mistakes become lessons, and our lives become adventures in growth, not stagnation.

God is able to take mistakes,
when they are committed to Him,
and make of them something for our good
and for His glory.

Ruth Bell Graham

— *A Prayer* —

Dear Lord, when I make mistakes, I will admit what I've done, and I will apologize to the people I've hurt. You are perfect, Lord; I am not. I thank You for Your forgiveness and for Your love.

Amen

New Beginnings

And He who sits on the throne said,
"Behold, I am making all things new."

Revelation 21:5 NASB

Create in me a pure heart, O God,
and renew a steadfast spirit within me.

Psalm 51:10 NIV

. . . inwardly we are being renewed day by day.

2 Corinthians 4:16 NIV

I will give you a new heart and put a new spirit in you . . . .

Ezekiel 36:26 NIV

Remember ye not the former things,
neither consider the things of old.
Behold, I will do a new thing . . . .

Isaiah 43:18, 19 KJV

*I*f we sincerely want to change ourselves for the better, we must start on the inside and work our way out from there. Lasting change doesn't occur "out there;" it occurs "in here." It occurs, not in the shifting sands of our own particular circumstances, but in quiet depths of our own hearts.

Are you in search of a new beginning or, for that matter, a new you? If so, don't expect changing circumstances to miraculously transform you into the person you want to become. Transformation starts with God, and it starts in the silent center of a humble human heart—like yours.

God is not running an antique shop!
He is making all things new!

Vance Havner

– A Prayer –

Dear Lord, You have the power to make all things new.
When I grow weary, let me turn my thoughts
and my prayers to You. When I am discouraged,
restore my faith in You. Renew my strength, Father,
and let me draw comfort and courage from
Your promises and from Your unending love.

Amen

Obedience

*Those who obey his commands live in him,
and he in them. And this is how we know that he lives in us:
We know it by the Spirit he gave us.*

1 John 3:24 NIV

*You shall walk after the LORD your God and fear Him,
and keep His commandments and obey His voice,
and you shall serve Him and hold fast to Him.*

Deuteronomy 13:4 NKJV

*Here is my final advice:
Honor God and obey his commands.*

Ecclesiastes 12:13 ICB

*If they obey and serve him, they will spend the rest of
their days in prosperity and their years in contentment.*

Job 36:11 NIV

*For it is not those who hear the law who are righteous in
God's sight, but it is those who obey the law
who will be declared righteous.*

Romans 2:13 NIV

*O*bedience to God is determined, not by words, but by deeds. Talking about righteousness is easy; living righteously is far more difficult, especially in today's temptation-filled world.

God has given us a guidebook for righteous living called the Holy Bible. It contains thorough instructions which, if followed, lead to fulfillment, righteousness and salvation. Unless we are willing to abide by God's laws, all of our righteous proclamations ring hollow. How, then, can we best proclaim our love for the Lord? By obeying Him. And, for further instructions, read the manual.

Rejoicing is a matter of obedience to God—
an obedience that will start you on the road to peace
and contentment.

Kay Arthur

— *A Prayer* —

Dear Lord, make me a woman who is obedient to
Your Word. Let me live according to
Your commandments. Direct my path far from
the temptations and distractions of this world.
And, let me discover Your will and follow it,
Lord, this day and always.

Amen

Patience

Patience is better than strength.

Proverbs 16:32 ICB

Patience and encouragement come from God.
And I pray that God will help you all agree
with each other the way Christ Jesus wants.

Romans 15:5 NCV

But if we look forward to something we don't have yet,
we must wait patiently and confidently.

Romans 8:25 NLT

The LORD is wonderfully good to those who wait for him
and seek him. So it is good to wait quietly
for salvation from the LORD.

Lamentations 3:25, 26 NLT

Wait on the LORD; Be of good courage,
and He shall strengthen your heart;
Wait, I say, on the LORD!

Psalm 27:14 NKJV

Psalm 37:7 commands us to wait patiently for God. But as busy women in a fast-paced world, many of us find that waiting quietly for God is difficult. Why? Because we are fallible human beings seeking to live according to our own timetables, not God's. In our better moments, we realize that patience is not only a virtue, it is also a commandment from God.

God instructs us to be patient in all things. We must be patient with our families, our friends, and our associates. We must also be patient with our Creator as He unfolds His plan for our lives. And that's as it should be. After all, think how patient God has been with us.

Wait on the Lord, wait patiently,
And thou shalt in Him be blest;
After the storm, a holy calm,
And after thy labor rest.

Fanny Crosby

– A Prayer –

Lord, sometimes I can be a very impatient person.
Slow me down and calm me down. Let me trust in
Your plan, Father; let me trust in Your timetable;
and let me trust in Your love for me.

Amen

Peace

God has called us to peace.

1 Corinthians 7:15 NKJV

Live peaceful and quiet lives in all godliness and holiness.

1 Timothy 2:2 NIV

*You, Lord, give true peace to those who depend on you,
because they trust you.*

Isaiah 26:3 NCV

*And the peace of God, which transcends all understanding,
will guard your hearts and your minds in Christ Jesus.*

Philippians 4:7 NIV

*Peace I leave with you, My peace I give to you;
not as the world gives do I give to you.
Let not your heart be troubled, neither let it be afraid.*

John 14:27 NKJV

The beautiful words of John 14:27 give us hope: "Peace I leave with you, my peace I give to you . . . ." Jesus offers us peace, not as the world gives, but as He alone gives. We, as believers, can accept His peace or ignore it. When we accept the peace of Jesus Christ into our hearts, our lives are transformed.

Christ's peace is offered freely; it has been paid for in full; it is ours for the asking. So let us ask . . . and then share.

O God, Thou hast made us for Thyself, and
our hearts are restless until they find their rest in Thee.

St. Augustine

– *A Prayer* –

Dear Lord, the peace that the world offers is fleeting,
but You offer a peace that is perfect and eternal.
Let me take my concerns and burdens to You, Father,
and let me feel the spiritual abundance that You offer
through the person of Your Son, the Prince of Peace.

Amen

Positive Outlook

Make me to hear joy and gladness . . . .

Psalm 51:8 KJV

My cup runs over. Surely goodness
and mercy shall follow me all the days of my life;
and I will dwell in the house of the LORD Forever.

Psalm 23:5, 6 NKJV

I can do everything through him that gives me strength.

Philippians 4:13 NIV

Finally, brethren, whatsoever things are true,
whatsoever things are honest, whatsoever things are just,
whatsoever things are pure, whatsoever things are lovely,
whatsoever things are of good report; if there be any virtue,
and if there be any praise, think on these things.

Philippians 4:8 KJV

*A*re you an optimistic, hopeful, enthusiastic Christian? You should be. After all, as a believer, you have every reason to be optimistic about life here on earth and life eternal. But sometimes, you may find yourself pulled down by the inevitable demands and worries of life here on earth. If you find yourself discouraged, exhausted, or both, then it's time to take your concerns to God.

Today, make this promise to yourself and keep it: Vow to be a hope-filled Christian. Think optimistically about your life, your profession, your family, and your future. Trust your hopes, not your fears. Take time to celebrate God's glorious creation. And then, when you've filled your heart with hope and gladness, share your optimism with others. They'll be better for it, and so will you.

The things we think are the things that feed our souls.
If we think on pure and lovely things,
we shall grow pure and lovely like them;
and the converse is equally true.

Hannah Whitall Smith

— A Prayer —
Lord, give me faith, optimism, and hope.
Let me expect the best from You, and let me look for the best in others. Let me trust You, Lord,
to direct my life. And, let me be Your faithful, hopeful, optimistic servant every day that I live.

Amen

Praise

I will praise You with my whole heart.

Psalm 138:1 NKJV

Is anyone happy? Let him sing songs of praise.

James 5:13 NIV

*Through Him then, let us continually offer up
a sacrifice of praise to God, that is,
the fruit of lips that give thanks to His name.*

Hebrews 13:15 NASB

*Praise ye the LORD. O give thanks unto the LORD;
for he is good: for his mercy endureth for ever.*

Psalm 106:1 KJV

*It is good to give thanks to the Lord, to sing praises to
the Most High. It is good to proclaim your unfailing love in
the morning, your faithfulness in the evening.*

Psalm 92:1, 2 NLT

The words by Fanny Crosby are familiar: "This is my story, this is my song, praising my Savior, all the day long." And, as believers who have been saved by the blood of a risen Christ, we must do exactly as the song instructs: We must praise our Savior many times each day.

Do you sincerely seek to be a worthy servant of the One who has given you eternal love and eternal life? Then praise Him for who He is and for what He has done for you. And don't just praise Him on Sunday morning. Praise Him all day long, every day, for as long as you live . . . and then for all eternity.

Praising God reduces your cares, levels your anxieties, and multiplies your blessings.

Suzanne Dale Ezell

– A Prayer –

Dear Lord, I come to You today with hope in my heart and praise on my lips. Make me a faithful steward of the blessings You have entrusted to me. Let me follow in Christ's footsteps today and every day that I live. And let my words and deeds praise You now and forever.

Amen

Problems

People who do what is right may have many problems,
but the Lord will solve them all.

Psalm 34:19 NCV

For when your faith is tested, your endurance
has a chance to grow. So let it grow, for when
your endurance is fully developed,
you will be strong in character and ready for anything.

James 1:3, 4 NLT

When you go through deep waters and great trouble,
I will be with you. When you go through the rivers of
difficulty, you will not drown! When you walk through
the fire of oppression, you will not be burned up;
the flames will not consume you.
For I am the LORD, your God . . . .

Isaiah 43:2, 3 NLT

Come to me, all you who are weary and burdened,
and I will give you rest. Take my yoke upon you
and learn from me, for I am gentle and humble in heart,
and you will find rest for your souls.
For my yoke is easy and my burden is light.

Matthew 11:28-30 NIV

*L*ife is an exercise in problem-solving. The question is not whether we will encounter problems; the real question is how we will choose to address them. When it comes to solving the problems of everyday living, we often know precisely what needs to be done, but we may be slow in doing it—especially if what needs to be done is difficult or uncomfortable for us. So we put off till tomorrow what should be done today.

What we see as problems God sees as opportunities. So today and every day, let us trust God by courageously confronting the things that we see as problems and He sees as possibilities.

God has plans—not problems—for our lives.
Before she died in the concentration camp in
Ravensbruck, my sister Betsie said to me,
"Corrie, your whole life has been a training for
the work you are doing here in prison—
and for the work you will do afterward."

Corrie ten Boom

— *A Prayer* —

Lord, sometimes my problems are simply too big
for me, but they are never too big for You. Let me turn
my troubles over to You, Lord, and let me trust
in You today and for all eternity.

Amen

Relationships

Do not be unequally yoked together with unbelievers.
For what fellowship has righteousness with lawlessness?
And what communion has light with darkness?

2 Corinthians 6:14 NKJV

Love does no harm to its neighbor.
Therefore love is the fulfillment of the law.

Romans 13:10 NIV

Thine own friend, and thy father's friend, forsake not . . . .

Proverbs 27:10 KJV

Carry each other's burdens,
and in this way you will fulfill the law of Christ.

Galatians 6:2 NIV

And be kind to one another, tenderhearted,
forgiving one another, just as God in Christ forgave you.

Ephesians 4:32 NKJV

How best do we build and maintain healthy relationships? By following the Word of God. Healthy relationships are built upon honesty, compassion, responsible behavior, trust, and optimism. Healthy relationships are built upon the Golden Rule. Healthy relationships are built upon sharing and caring. All of these principles are found time and time again in God's Holy Word. When we read God's Word and follow His commandments, we enrich our own lives and the lives of those who are closest to us.

The single most important element
in any human relationship is honesty—
with oneself, with God, and with others.

Catherine Marshall

— A Prayer —

Dear Lord, You have brought family members
and friends into my life. Let me love them,
let me help them, let me treasure them,
and let me lead them to You.

Amen

Sad Days

You will be sad, but your sadness will become joy.

John 16:20 NCV

*He was despised and rejected by men, a man of sorrows,
and familiar with suffering.*

Isaiah 53:3 NIV

*But may the God of all grace, who called us
to His eternal glory by Christ Jesus,
after you have suffered a while,
perfect, establish, strengthen, and settle you.*

1 Peter 5:10 NKJV

For whatsoever is born of God overcometh the world . . . .

1 John 5:4 KJV

*We are hard pressed on every side, but not crushed;
perplexed, but not in despair . . . .*

2 Corinthians 4:8 NIV

*Then they cried unto the LORD in their trouble,
and he saved them out of their distresses.*

Psalm 107:13 KJV

Women of every generation have experienced adversity, and this generation is no different. But, today's women face challenges that previous generations could have scarcely imagined. Thankfully, although the world continues to change, God's love remains constant.

Some days are light and happy, and some days are not. When we face the inevitable dark days of life, we must choose how we will respond. Will we allow ourselves to sink even more deeply into our own sadness, or will we do the difficult work of pulling ourselves out? We bring light to the dark days of life by turning first to God, and then to trusted family members and friends. Then, we must go to work solving the problems that confront us. When we do, the clouds will eventually part, and the sun will shine once more upon our souls.

The best way to show my gratitude to God
is to accept everything, even my problems, with joy.

Mother Teresa

– *A Prayer* –

Lord, sometimes our hearts are broken,
but even then You never leave us. On sad days,
I will turn my thoughts and my prayers to You, and
in Your own time and according to Your perfect plan,
You will heal my broken heart.

Amen

Salvation

Sing to the LORD, all the earth;
proclaim his salvation day after day.

1 Chronicles 16:23 NIV

Blessed be the God and Father of our Lord Jesus Christ,
who according to His great mercy has caused us
to be born again to a living hope through
the resurrection of Jesus Christ from the dead.

1 Peter 1:3 NASB

And there is salvation in no one else;
for there is no other name under heaven that has been given
among men by which we must be saved.

Acts 4:12 NASB

And we have seen and testify that the Father
has sent his Son to be the Savior of the world.

1 John 4:14 NIV

For there is one God and one mediator between God and
men, the man Christ Jesus,
who gave himself as a ransom for all men . . . .

1 Timothy 2:5, 6 NIV

Christ sacrificed His life on the cross so that we might have eternal life. This gift, freely given by God's only begotten Son, is the priceless possession of everyone who accepts Him as Lord and Savior. God is waiting patiently for each of us to accept the gift of eternal life. Let us claim Christ's gift today.

It is by God's grace that we have been saved, through faith. We are saved not because of our good deeds but because of our faith in Christ. May we, who have been given so much, praise our Savior for the gift of salvation, and may we share the joyous news of our Master's love and His grace.

I now know the power of the risen Lord! He lives!
The dawn of Easter has broken in my own soul!
My night is gone!

Mrs. Charles E. Cowman

– A Prayer –

Lord, I'm only here on earth for a brief visit.
Heaven is my real home. You've given me the gift of
eternal life through Your Son Jesus. I accept Your gift,
Lord. And I will share Your Good News so that
my family and friends, too, might come to know
Christ's healing touch.

Amen

Scripture

There's nothing like the written Word of God for showing
you the way to salvation through faith in Christ Jesus.
Every part of Scripture is God-breathed and useful one
way or another, showing us truth, exposing our rebellion,
correcting our mistakes, training us to live God's way.
Through the Word we are put together and
shaped up for the tasks God has for us.

2 Timothy 3:15-17 MSG

Your word is a lamp to my feet and a light to my path.

Psalm 119:105 NKJV

Heaven and earth will pass away,
but my words will never pass away.

Matthew 24:35 NIV

Jesus answered, "It is written:
'Man does not live by bread alone,
but on every word that comes from the mouth of God.'"

Matthew 4:4 NIV

s God's Word a lamp that guides your path? Is God's Word your indispensable compass for everyday living, or is it relegated to Sunday morning services? Do you read the Bible faithfully or sporadically? The answer to these questions will determine the direction of your thoughts, the direction of your day, and the direction of your life.

God's Word can be a roadmap to a place of righteous and abundance. Make it your roadmap. God's wisdom can be a light to guide your steps. Claim it as your light today, tomorrow, and every day of your life—and then walk confidently in the footsteps of God's only begotten Son.

Decisions which are made in the light of
God's Word are stable and show wisdom.

Vonette Z. Bright

– A Prayer –

Dear Lord, Your scripture is a light unto the world;
let me study it, trust it, and share it with all who cross
my path. In all that I do, help me be a woman who is
a worthy witness for You as I share the Good News of
Your perfect Son and Your perfect Word.

Amen

Seeking God

I sought the LORD, and He heard me,
and delivered me from all my fears.

Psalm 34:4 NKJV

The LORD is good to those whose hope is in him,
to the one who seeks him . . . .

Lamentations 3:25 NIV

Seek the LORD while he may be found;
call on him while he is near.

Isaiah 55:6 NIV

I seek you with all my heart;
do not let me stray from your commands.

Psalm 119:10 NIV

But seek first the kingdom of God and His righteousness,
and all these things shall be added to you.

Matthew 6:33 NKJV

The familiar words of Matthew 6 remind us that, as believers, we must seek God and His Kingdom. And when we seek Him with our hearts open and our prayers lifted, we need not look far: God is with us always.

Sometimes, in the crush of your daily duties, God may seem far away. Or sometimes, when the disappointments and sorrows of life leave you breathless, God may seem distant, but He is not. When you earnestly seek God, you will find Him because He is here, waiting patiently for you to reach out to Him . . . right here . . . right now.

Joy is available to all who seek His riches.
The key to joy is found in the person
of Jesus Christ and in His will.

Kay Arthur

– A Prayer –
Dear Lord, in the quiet moments of this day,
I will turn my thoughts and prayers to You.
In these silent moments, I will seek Your presence,
and Your will for my life, knowing that when
I accept Your peace, I will be blessed today
and throughout eternity.
Amen

Serving Others

So prepare your minds for service and have self-control.

1 Peter 1:13 NCV

Let this mind be in you which was also in Christ Jesus,
who . . . made Himself of no reputation, taking the form
of a bondservant, and coming in the likeness of men.

Philippians 2:5, 7 NKJV

Therefore, since we receive a kingdom which cannot be
shaken, let us show gratitude, by which we may offer
to God an acceptable service with reverence and awe . . . .

Hebrews 12:28 NASB

Suppose a brother or a sister is without clothes and daily
food. If one of you says to him, "Go, I wish you well;
keep warm and well fed," but does nothing about
his physical needs, what good is it?

James 2:15, 16 NIV

But a Samaritan, as he traveled, came where the man was;
and when he saw him, he took pity on him.
He went to him and bandaged his wounds, pouring on oil
and wine. Then he put the man on his own donkey,
took him to an inn and took care of him.

Luke 10:33, 34 NIV

*I*f you genuinely seek to discover God's unfolding purpose for your life, you must ask yourself this question: "How does God want me to serve others?"

Every single day of your life, including this one, God will give you opportunities to serve Him by serving His children. Welcome those opportunities with open arms. They are God's gift to you, His way of allowing you to achieve greatness in His Kingdom.

We can love Jesus in the hungry, the naked, and
the destitute who are dying . . . If you love, you will be
willing to serve. And you will find Jesus in
the distressing disguise of the poor.

Mother Teresa

– *A Prayer* –

Dear Lord, in weak moments, I seek to build
myself up by placing myself ahead of others.
But Your commandment, Father, is that I become
a humble servant to those who need my
encouragement, my help, and my love. Create in me
a servant's heart. And, let be a woman who follows
in the footsteps of Your Son Jesus who taught us by
example that to be great in Your eyes, Lord,
is to serve others humbly, faithfully, and lovingly.

Amen

Sharing

The one who blesses others is abundantly blessed;
those who help others are helped.

Proverbs 11:25 MSG

Shepherd God's flock, for whom you are responsible.
Watch over them because you want to,
not because you are forced. That is how God wants it.
Do it because you are happy to serve.

1 Peter 5:2 NCV

In everything I did, I showed you that by this kind of hard
work we must help the weak, remembering the words
the Lord Jesus himself said:
"It is more blessed to give than to receive."

Acts 20:35 NIV

He that hath two coats, let him impart to him that hath none;
and he that hath meat, let him do likewise.

Luke 3:11 KJV

We live in a fast-paced, competitive world where it is easy to say, "Me first." But, God instructs us to do otherwise. In God's Kingdom, those who proclaim, "Me first," are last. God loves a cheerful, selfless giver. If we seek greatness in God's eyes, we must look our neighbors squarely in the eye and say, "You first." When we do, we will follow in the footsteps of the humble servant who died for our sins: Christ Jesus.

When somebody needs a helping hand, he doesn't need
it tomorrow or the next day. He needs it now,
and that's exactly when you should offer to help.
Good deeds, if they are really good,
happen sooner rather than later.

Marie T. Freeman

— *A Prayer* —

Dear Lord, sometimes it's easy to think only of myself,
and not of others. Help me remember that
I should treat other people in the same way that
I would want to be treated if I were standing in
their shoes. You have given me many blessings,
Lord—let me share them now.

Amen

Strength

Be of good courage, and let us be strong for our people
and for the cities of our God.
And may the LORD do what is good in His sight.

1 Chronicles 19:13 NKJV

Do you not know? Have you not heard?
The Everlasting God, the LORD, the Creator of
the ends of the earth does not become weary or tired.
His understanding is inscrutable. He gives strength to
the weary, and to him who lacks might He increases power.
Though youths grow weary and tired, and vigorous young
men stumble badly, yet those who wait for
the LORD will gain new strength; they will mount up
with wings like eagles, they will run and not get tired,
they will walk and not become weary.

Isaiah 40:28-31 NASB

He said unto me, My grace is sufficient for thee:
for my strength is made perfect in weakness.

2 Corinthians 12:9 KJV

The LORD is my strength and my song . . . .

Exodus 15:2 NIV

All of us must endure difficult days when our trust is tested and our strength is sapped. Thankfully, even on the darkest days, we need not endure our troubles alone. God's Word promises that He will renew our strength when we offer our hearts and prayers to Him.

Today, invite God into your heart and allow Him to renew your spirits. When you trust Him and Him alone, He will never fail you. Life can be challenging, but fear not. God loves you, and He will protect you. Whatever your challenge, God can handle it. Let Him.

> The strength that we claim from God's Word
> does not depend on circumstances.
> Circumstances will be difficult,
> but our strength will be sufficient.
>
> *Corrie ten Boom*

— *A Prayer* —

Dear Heavenly Father, You are my strength.
When I am troubled, You comfort me.
When I am discouraged, You lift me up. When I am
afraid, You deliver me. Let me turn to You, Lord, when
I am weak. In times of hardship, let me trust Your plan,
Lord, and whatever my circumstances,
let me look to You for my strength and my salvation.

Amen

Stress

"LORD, help!" they cried in their trouble,
and he saved them from their distress.

Psalm 107:13 NLT

You have allowed me to suffer much hardship,
but you will restore me to life again and lift me up from
the depths of the earth. You will restore me to
even greater honor and comfort me once again.

Psalm 71:20, 21 NLT

When my heart is overwhelmed:
lead me to the rock that is higher than I.

Psalm 61:2 KJV

God, who comforts the downcast, comforted us . . . .

2 Corinthians 7:6 NIV

Be strong and brave, and do the work.
Don't be afraid or discouraged, because the Lord God,
my God, is with you. He will not fail you or leave you.

1 Chronicles 28:20 NCV

*E*very woman knows that stressful days are an inevitable fact of modern life. And how do we deal with the challenges of being a busy female in a demanding, 21st-century world? By turning our days and our lives over to God. Elisabeth Elliot writes, "If my life is surrendered to God, all is well. Let me not grab it back, as though it were in peril in His hand but would be safer in mine!" May we give our lives, our hopes, and our prayers to the Father, and, by doing so, accept His will and His peace.

Don't be overwhelmed . . .
take it one day and one prayer at a time.

Stormie Omartian

– A Prayer –

Lord, sometimes life is difficult. Sometimes,
I am worried, weary, or discouraged.
But, when I lift my eyes to You, Father,
You strengthen me. Today, I will turn to You, Lord,
for strength, for hope, and for salvation.

Amen

Talking to God

The intense prayer of the righteous is very powerful.

James 5:16 HCSB

For I know the thoughts that I think toward you,
says the LORD, thoughts of peace and not of evil,
to give you a future and a hope. Then you will call upon
Me and go and pray to Me, and I will listen to you.

Jeremiah 29:11, 12 NKJV

Do not be anxious about anything, but in everything,
by prayer and petition, with thanksgiving,
present your requests to God.

Philippians 4:6 NIV

Watch therefore, and pray always.

Luke 21:36 NKJV

If my people who are called by my name,
will humble themselves and pray and seek my face
and turn from their wicked ways, then will I hear from
heaven and will forgive their sin and will heal their land.

2 Chronicles 7:14 NIV

*I*s prayer an integral part of your daily life or is it a hit-or-miss habit? Do you "pray without ceasing," or is your prayer life an afterthought? Do you regularly pray in the solitude of the early morning hours, or do you bow your head only when others are watching?

The quality of your spiritual life will be in direct proportion to the quality of your prayer life. Prayer changes things, and it changes you. Today, instead of turning things over in your mind, turn them over to God in prayer. Instead of worrying about your next decision, ask God to lead the way. Don't limit your prayers to meals or to bedtime. Pray constantly about things great and small. God is listening, and He wants to hear from you.

We must pray literally without ceasing,
in every occurrence and employment of our lives.
You know I mean that prayer of the heart which is
independent of place or situation, or which is, rather,
a habit of lifting up the heart to God,
as in a constant communication with Him.

Elizabeth Ann Seton

— *A Prayer* —
Dear Lord, I will be a woman of prayer.
I will take everything to You in prayer,
and when I do, I will trust Your answers.

Amen

Temper

Patient people have great understanding,
but people with quick tempers show their foolishness.

Proverbs 14:29 NCV

A hot-tempered man stirs up dissention,
but a patient man calms a quarrel.

Proverbs 15:18 NIV

Now you must rid yourselves of all such things as these:
anger, rage, malice . . . .

Colossians 3:8 NIV

Refrain from anger and turn from wrath;
do not fret—it leads only to evil.

Psalm 37:8 NIV

Do not let the sun go down on your anger,
and do not give the devil an opportunity.

Ephesians 4:26, 27 NASB

Your temper is either your master or your servant. Either you control it, or it controls you. And the extent to which you allow anger to rule your life will determine, to a surprising extent, the quality of your relationships with others and your relationship with God.

Anger and peace cannot coexist in the same mind. If you allow yourself to be chronically angry, you must forfeit the peace that might otherwise be yours through Christ. So obey God's Word by turning away from anger today and every day. You'll be glad you did, and so will your family and friends.

Why lose your temper if, by doing so, you offend God,
annoy other people, give yourself a bad time . . .
and, in the end, have to find it again?

Josemaria Escriva

– A Prayer –

Lord, sometimes, in moments of frustration,
my temper flares. When I fall prey to pettiness,
restore my sense of perspective. When I fall prey to
irrational anger, give me inner calm. Let me show
my thankfulness to You by offering forgiveness to others.
And, when I do, may others see Your love reflected
through my words and my deeds.

Amen

Thanksgiving

Thanks be to God for His indescribable gift!

2 Corinthians 9:15 NKJV

Give thanks in all circumstances;
for this is God's will for you in Christ Jesus.

1 Thessalonians 5:18 NIV

Make a joyful noise unto the LORD all ye lands.
Serve the LORD with gladness: come before his presence
with singing. Know ye that the LORD he is God: it is he
that hath made us, and not we ourselves; we are his people
and the sheep of his pasture. Enter into his gates with
thanksgiving, and into his courts with praise;
be thankful unto him and bless his name.
For the LORD is good; his mercy is everlasting;
and his truth endureth to all generations.

Psalm 100 KJV

I will thank you, LORD, with all my heart;
I will tell of all the marvelous things you have done.
I will be filled with joy because of you.
I will sing praises to your name, O Most High.

Psalm 9:1, 2 NLT

*S*ometimes, life here on earth can be complicated, demanding, and frustrating. When the demands of life leave us rushing from place to place with scarcely a moment to spare, we may fail to pause and thank our Creator for the countless blessings He bestows upon us. But, whenever we neglect to give proper thanks to the Giver of all things good, we suffer because of our misplaced priorities.

Are you taking God's gifts for granted? If so, you are doing a disservice to your Creator and to yourself. And the best way to resolve that problem is to make this day a time for celebration and praise. Starting now.

God is worthy of our praise and is pleased
when we come before Him with thanksgiving.

Shirley Dobson

– *A Prayer* –
Lord, let me be a thankful Christian.
Your blessings are priceless and eternal.
I praise You, Lord, for Your gifts and,
most of all, for Your Son.
Amen

Today

*While it is daytime, we must continue doing
the work of the One who sent me.
Night is coming, when no one can work.*

John 9:4 NCV

*For he says, "In the time of my favor I heard you,
and in the day of salvation I helped you." I tell you,
now is the time of God's favor, now is the day of salvation.*

2 Corinthians 6:2 NIV

*Encourage one another daily,
as long as it is called Today . . . .*

Hebrews 3:13 NIV

*Give your entire attention to what God is doing right now,
and don't get worked up about what may or
may not happen tomorrow. God will help you deal
with whatever hard things come up when the time comes.*

Matthew 6:34 MSG

*This is the day which the LORD has made;
let us rejoice and be glad in it.*

Psalm 118:24 NASB

The familiar words of Psalm 118:24 remind us that every day is a gift from God. Yet on some days, we don't feel much like celebrating. When the obligations of everyday living seem to overwhelm us, we may find ourselves frustrated by the demands of the present and worried by the uncertainty of the future.

Each day is a special treasure to be savored and celebrated. May we—as believers who have so much to celebrate—never fail to praise our Creator by rejoicing in His glorious creation.

Today is mine. Tomorrow is none of my business.
If I peer anxiously into the fog of the future,
I will strain my spiritual eyes so that
I will not see clearly what is required of me now.

Elisabeth Elliot

– A Prayer –

This is the day that You have given me, Lord.
Let me be thankful, and let me use it according to
Your plan. I praise You, Father, for the gift of life and
for the friends and family members who make
my life rich. Enable me to live each moment to
the fullest, totally involved in Your will.

Amen

Trusting God

And God, in his mighty power, will protect you until
you receive this salvation, because you are trusting him.

1 Peter 1:5 NLT

For we walk by faith, not by sight.

2 Corinthians 5:7 NASB

Do not let your hearts be troubled. Trust in God;
trust also in me. In my Father's house are many rooms;
if it were not so, I would have told you.
I am going there to prepare a place for you.

John 14:1, 2 NIV

It is better to trust in the LORD than to put confidence
in man. It is better to trust in the LORD
than to put confidence in princes.

Psalm 118:8, 9 KJV

Trust the LORD your God with all your heart and
lean not on your own understanding;
in all your ways acknowledge him,
and he will make your paths straight.

Proverbs 3:5, 6 NIV

*I*f we believe in God, we should trust in God. Yet sometimes, when we are besieged by fears and doubts, trusting God is hard indeed.

Are you willing to trust God completely, or are you still sitting squarely on the spiritual fence? The answer to this question will determine the tone, the quality, and the direction of your life. When you trust your Heavenly Father without reservation, you can be sure that, in His own fashion and in His own time, God will bless you in ways that you never could have imagined. So trust Him. And then prepare yourself for the abundance and the joy that will most certainly be yours when you do.

Make the least of all that goes and the most of all
that comes. Don't regret what is past.
Cherish what you have. Look forward to all
that is to come. And most important of all,
rely moment by moment on Jesus Christ.

Gigi Graham Tchividjian

– A Prayer –

Dear Lord, even when I don't understand why things
happen, I will trust You. Even when I am confused or
worried, I will trust You. There are many things that
I cannot do, Lord, and there are many things that
I cannot understand. But one thing
I can do is to trust You always. And I will.

Amen

Truth

And you shall know the truth,
and the truth shall make you free.

John 8:32 NKJV

Jesus said to him, "I am the way, the truth, and the life.
No one comes to the Father except through Me.
If you had known Me, you would have known
My Father also; and from now on you know Him
and have seen Him."

John 14:6, 7 NKJV

I have no greater joy than to hear
that my children walk in truth.

3 John 1:4 KJV

A person who does not have the Spirit does not accept
the truths that come from the Spirit of God.
That person thinks they are foolish and cannot understand
them, because they can only be judged to be true by
the Spirit. The spiritual person is able to judge all things,
but no one can judge him.

1 Corinthians 2:14, 15 NCV

God is vitally concerned with truth. His Word teaches the truth; His Spirit reveals the truth; His Son leads us to the truth. When we open our hearts to God, and when we allow His Son to rule over our thoughts and our lives, God reveals Himself, and we come to understand the truth about ourselves and the Truth about God's gift of grace.

The familiar words of John 8:32 remind us that God's truth has the power to set us free. May we, as believers, seek God's truth and live by it, this day and forever.

God will see to it that we understand
as much truth as we are willing to obey.

Elisabeth Elliot

— A Prayer —

Heavenly Father, You are the way and the truth and
the light. Today, as I follow Your way, and live in
Your truth, and share Your light with others,
I thank You for the inevitable result in my life:
freedom.

Amen

Wisdom

Therefore everyone who hears these words of mine
and puts them into practice is like a wise man
who built his house on the rock.

Matthew 7:24 NIV

But the wisdom that is from above is first pure,
then peaceable, gentle, willing to yield, full of mercy and
good fruits, without partiality and without hypocrisy.

James 3:17 NKJV

Who is wise and understanding among you?
Let him show by good conduct that his works
are done in the meekness of wisdom.

James 3:13 NKJV

Let the word of Christ dwell in you richly in all wisdom;
teaching and admonishing one another in psalms and
hymns and spiritual songs,
singing with grace in your hearts to the Lord.

Colossians 3:16 KJV

The fear of the LORD is the beginning of wisdom,
and knowledge of the Holy One is understanding.

Proverbs 9:10 NIV

*D*o you seek wisdom for yourself and for your family? Of course you do. But as a savvy woman, you know that wisdom can be an elusive commodity in today's troubled world. In a society filled with temptations and distractions; it's easy to stray far from the source of the ultimate wisdom: God's Holy Word.

Wisdom is not like a mushroom; it does not spring up overnight. It is, instead, like an oak tree that starts as a tiny acorn, grows into a sapling, and eventually reaches up to the sky, tall and strong. So today, as a way of understanding God's plan for your life, study His Word and live by it. When you do, you will accumulate a storehouse of wisdom that will enrich your own life and the lives of your family members, your friends, and the world.

Wisdom is knowledge applied. Head knowledge is useless on the battlefield. Knowledge stamped on the heart makes one wise.

Beth Moore

– *A Prayer* –

Lord, make me a woman of wisdom and discernment.
I seek wisdom, Lord, not as the world gives,
but as You give. Lead me in Your ways and teach me
from Your Word so that, in time, my wisdom
might glorify Your Kingdom and Your Son.
Amen

Witness

We are therefore Christ's ambassadors,
as though God were making his appeal through us.
We implore you on Christ's behalf: Be reconciled to God.

2 Corinthians 5:20 NIV

You are the light of the world. A city that is set on
a hill cannot be hidden. Nor do they light a lamp and
put it under a basket, but on a lampstand,
and it gives light to all who are in the house.
Let your light so shine before men, that they may see
your good works and glorify your Father in heaven.

Matthew 5:14-16 NKJV

Sanctify the Lord God in your hearts:
and be ready always to give an answer to every man
that asketh you a reason of the hope that is in you . . . .

1 Peter 3:15 KJV

And I say to you, everyone who confesses Me before men,
the Son of Man will confess him also
before the angels of God . . . .

Luke 12:8 NASB

*I*n his second letter to Timothy, Paul offers a message to believers of every generation when he writes, "God has not given us a spirit of timidity." Paul's meaning is clear: When witnessing to others, we must be courageous, forthright, and unashamed.

We live in a world that desperately needs the healing message of Christ Jesus. Every believer, each in his or her own way, bears a personal responsibility for sharing that message. If you are a believer in Christ, you know how He has touched your heart and changed your life. Now it's your turn to share the Good News with others. And remember: Today is the perfect time to share your testimony because tomorrow may quite simply be too late.

> When you are sold out to God,
> you cannot not go and tell.
>
> *Liz Curtis Higgs*

— A Prayer —

Dear Lord, let me share the Good News of
Your Son Jesus. Let the life that I live and the words
that I speak bear witness to my faith in Him.
And let me share the story of my salvation
with others so that they, too, might dedicate their lives
to Christ and receive His eternal gifts.

Amen

Work

But one thing I do: Forgetting what is behind
and straining toward what is ahead,
I press on toward the goal to win the prize for which
God has called me heavenward in Christ Jesus.

Philippians 3:13, 14 NIV

Then He said to His disciples,
"The harvest truly is plentiful, but the laborers are few."

Matthew 9:37 NKJV

The people had a mind to work.

Nehemiah 4:6 KJV

But as for you, be strong and do not give up,
for your work will be rewarded.

2 Chronicles 15:7 NIV

Work hard so God can approve you.
Be a good worker, one who does not need to be ashamed
and who correctly explains the word of truth.

2 Timothy 2:15 NLT

The old adage is both familiar and true: We must pray as if everything depended upon God, but work as if everything depended upon us.

It has been said that there are no shortcuts to any place worth going. Women agree. Making the grade in today's competitive world is not easy. But, even when the workday is long and the workload is difficult, we must not become discouraged. God did not create us for lives of mediocrity; He created us for far greater things. Earning great things usually requires work and lots of it, which is perfectly fine with God. After all, He knows that we're up to the task, and He has big plans for us. Very big plans.

> I long to accomplish a great and noble task,
> but it is my chief duty to accomplish small tasks
> as if they were great and noble.
>
> *Helen Keller*

– A Prayer –

Heavenly Father, I seek to be Your faithful servant.
When I am tired, give me strength. When I become
frustrated, give me patience. When I lose sight of
Your purpose for my life, give me a passion for my daily
responsibilities, and when I have completed my work,
let all the honor and glory be Yours.

Amen

Worry

Jesus said, "Don't let your hearts be troubled.
Trust in God, and trust in me."

John 14:1 NCV

Come to Me, all you who labor and are heavy laden, and
I will give you rest. Take My yoke upon you and learn from
Me, for I am gentle and lowly in heart, and you will find rest
for your souls. For My yoke is easy and My burden is light.

Matthew 11:28-30 NKJV

So don't worry, saying, "What will we eat?" or
"What will we drink?" or "What will we wear?"
For the Gentiles eagerly seek all these things, and your
heavenly Father knows that you need them. But seek first
the kingdom of God and His righteousness, and all these
things will be provided for you. Therefore don't worry about
tomorrow, because tomorrow will worry about itself.
Each day has enough trouble of its own.

Matthew 6:31-34 HCSB

Yea, though I walk through the valley of the shadow of death,
I will fear no evil: for thou art with me;
thy rod and thy staff they comfort me.

Psalm 23:4 KJV

ecause we are fallible human beings, we worry. Even though we, as Christians, have the assurance of salvation—even though we, as Christians, have the promise of God's love and protection—we find ourselves fretting over the countless details of everyday life.

If you are like most women, you may, on occasion, find yourself worrying about health, about finances, about safety, about relationships, about family, and about countless other challenges of life, some great and some small. Where is the best place to take your worries? Take them to God. Take your troubles to Him, and your fears, and your sorrows. And remember: God is trustworthy . . . and you are protected.

Any concern that is too small to be turned into
a prayer is too small to be made into a burden.

Corrie ten Boom

— *A Prayer* —

Lord, sometimes this world is an intimidating place.
I may worry about my family, my job, or my health.
And when I do, my worries sap my strength. Lord,
fill me with your Spirit, and let me not be timid as
I face the opportunities and challenges of today
by trusting completely in You.

Amen

Worship

Worship the Lord your God and . . . serve Him only.

Matthew 4:10 HCSB

God lifted him high and honored him far beyond anyone or
anything, ever, so that all created beings in heaven and earth,
even those long ago dead and buried, will bow in worship
before this Jesus Christ, and call out in praise that he is
the Master of all, to the glorious honor of God the Father.

Philippians 2:9-11 MSG

Worship the LORD with gladness. Come before him,
singing with joy. Acknowledge that the LORD is God!
He made us, and we are his.
We are his people, the sheep of his pasture.

Psalm 100:2, 3 NLT

A time is coming and has now come when the true
worshipers will worship the Father in spirit and truth, for they
are the kind of worshipers the Father seeks. God is spirit,
and his worshipers must worship in spirit and in truth.

John 4:23, 24 NIV

All the earth shall worship thee, and shall sing unto thee;
they shall sing to thy name . . . .

Psalm 66:4 KJV

When we worship God faithfully and fervently, we are blessed. When we fail to worship God, for whatever reason, we forfeit the spiritual gifts that He intends for us.

We must worship our heavenly Father, not just with our words, but also with deeds. We must honor Him, praise Him, and obey Him. As we seek to find purpose and meaning for our lives, we must first seek His purpose and His will. For believers, God comes first. Always first.

Worship always empowers the worshiper with a greater revelation of the object of her desire.

Lisa Bevere

— *A Prayer* —

When I worship You, Dear Lord, You set my path—and my heart—straight. Let this day and every day be a time of worship. Whether I am in Your house or simply going about my daily activities, let me worship You, not only with words and deeds, but also with my heart. In the quiet moments of the day, I will praise You for creating me, loving me, guiding me, and saving me.

Amen